# Journal

## of
## Soviet and Post-Soviet
## Politics and Society

Vol. 4, No. 2 (2018)

Special Section

# Issues in the History and Memory of the OUN II

JSPPS 4:2 (2018)

GENERAL EDITOR AND ISSUE EDITOR-IN-CHIEF:

**Julie Fedor,** University of Melbourne

GUEST EDITORS:

**Andreas Umland,** Institute for Euro-Atlantic Cooperation, Kyiv

**Yuliya Yurchuk,** Södertörn University, Sweden

# JSPPS Editorial Team

Julie Fedor, *University of Melbourne* (General Editor)
Andrey Makarychev, *University of Tartu* (Editor)
Gergana Dimova, *University of Winchester* (Reviews Editor)
Andreas Umland, *Institute for Euro-Atlantic Cooperation, Kyiv* (Consulting Editor)

## JSPPS Advisory Board

Hannes Adomeit, College of Europe, Natolin
Timofey Agarin, Queen's University, Belfast
Mikhail Alexseev, San Diego State University, CA
Catherine Andreyev, University of Oxford
Anne Applebaum, The Legatum Institute, London
Anders Åslund, Peterson Inst. for International Economics
Margarita Balmaceda, Seton Hall University, NJ
Harley Balzer, Georgetown University, DC
John Barber, University of Cambridge
Timm Beichelt, European University Viadrina, Frankfurt (Oder)
Mark R. Beissinger, Princeton University, NJ
Thomas Bohn, Justus Liebig University, Giessen
Giovanna Brogi, University of Milan
Paul Chaisty, University of Oxford
Vitaly Chernetsky, University of Kansas, Lawrence
Ariel Cohen, Institute for the Analysis of Global Security, MD
Timothy J. Colton, Harvard University, MA
Peter J.S. Duncan, University College London
John B. Dunlop, Stanford University, CA
Gerald M. Easter, Boston College, MA
Alexander Etkind, European University Institute, Florence
M. Steven Fish, University of California at Berkeley
Gasan Gusejnov, Higher School of Economics, Moscow
Nikolas K. Gvosdev, U.S. Naval War College, RI
Michael Hagemeister, Ruhr University, Bochum
Stephen E. Hanson, College of William & Mary, VA
Olexiy Haran, Kyiv-Mohyla Academy
Nicolas Hayoz, University of Fribourg
Andreas Heinemann-Grüder, University of Bonn
Stephen Hutchings, University of Manchester, UK
Stefani Hoffman, The Hebrew University of Jerusalem
Mikhail Ilyin, Higher School of Economics, Moscow
Wilfried Jilge, University of Basel
Markku Kangaspuro, University of Helsinki
Adrian Karatnycky, Atlantic Council, New York
Andrei Kazantsev, MGIMO, Moscow

Jeffrey Kopstein, University of Toronto
Hrant Kostanyan, Centre for European Policy Studies
Paul Kubicek, Oakland University, MI
Walter Laqueur, Georgetown University, DC
Marlene Laruelle, George Washington University, DC
Carol Leonard, Higher School of Economics, Moscow
Leonid Luks, The Catholic University of Eichstaett-Ingolstadt
Luke March, University of Edinburgh
Mykhailo Minakov, Kyiv-Mohyla Academy
Olga Onuch, University of Manchester
Mitchell Orenstein, Northeastern University, MA
Nikolay Petrov, Higher School of Economics, Moscow
Andriy Portnov, Humboldt University, Berlin
Serhii Plokhii, Harvard University, MA
Alina Polyakova, Atlantic Council, DC
Maria Popova, McGill University, Montreal
Alex Pravda, University of Oxford
Mykola Riabchuk, Ukrainian Academy of Sciences, Kyiv
Per Anders Rudling, Lund University
Ellen Rutten, University of Amsterdam
Jutta Scherrer, École des Hautes Études en Sciences Sociales
Dieter Segert, University of Vienna
Anton Shekhovtsov, The Legatum Institute, London
Oxana Shevel, Tufts University, MA
Stephen Shulman, Southern Illinois University, Carbondale
Valerie Sperling, Clark University, MA
Susan Stewart, SWP, Berlin
Lisa M. Sundstrom, University of British Columbia
Mark Tauger, West Virginia University, Morgantown
Vera Tolz-Zilitinkevic, University of Manchester
Amir Weiner, Stanford University
Sarah Whitmore, Oxford Brookes University, UK
Andrew Wilson, University College London
Christian Wipperfürth, DGAP, Berlin
Andreas Wittkowsky, ZIF, Berlin
Jan Zielonka, University of Oxford

**Bibliographic information published by the Deutsche Nationalbibliothek**
The Deutsche Nationalbibliothek lists this publication in the Deutsche Nationalbibliografie; detailed bibliographic data are available on the Internet at http://dnb.dnb.de.

**Bibliografische Information der Deutschen Nationalbibliothek**
Die Deutsche Nationalbibliothek verzeichnet diese Publikation in der Deutschen Nationalbibliografie; detaillierte bibliografische Daten sind im Internet über http://dnb.d-nb.de abrufbar.

Cover picture:   Emblem of OUN.
Source: © Alex Tora via Wikimedia Commons. Licensed under CC BY 3.0 (s. https://creativecommons.org/licenses/by/3.0/deed.en).

**Journal of Soviet and Post-Soviet Politics and Society**
**Vol. 4, No. 2 (2018)**

Stuttgart: *ibidem*-Verlag / *ibidem* Press

Erscheinungsweise: halbjährlich / Frequency: biannual

ISSN 2364-5334

**Ordering Information:**
PRINT: Subscription (two copies per year): € 58.00 / year (+ S&H: € 4.00 / year within Germany, € 7.00 / year international). The subscription can be canceled at any time.

Single copy or back issue: € 34.00 / copy (+ S&H: € 2.00 within Germany, € 3.50 international).

E-BOOK: Individual copy or back issue: € 19.99 / copy. Available via amazon.com or google.books.

For further information please visit www.jspps.eu

© *ibidem*-Verlag / *ibidem* Press
Stuttgart, Germany 2018

Alle Rechte vorbehalten
Das Werk einschließlich aller seiner Teile ist urheberrechtlich geschützt. Jede Verwertung außerhalb der engen Grenzen des Urheberrechtsgesetzes ist ohne Zustimmung des Verlages unzulässig und strafbar. Dies gilt insbesondere für Vervielfältigungen, Übersetzungen, Mikroverfilmungen und elektronische Speicherformen sowie die Einspeicherung und Verarbeitung in elektronischen Systemen.

All rights reserved

No part of this publication may be reproduced, stored in or introduced into a retrieval system, or transmitted, in any form, or by any means (electronic, mechanical, photocopying, recording or otherwise) without the prior written permission of the publisher.
Any person who performs any unauthorized act in relation to this publication may be liable to criminal prosecution and civil claims for damages.

Printed in the EU

# CONTENTS

Soviet Bureaucracy as a Category Coining Machine: Ethnicity, Ethnography, and the "Primordial Trap"
SIMON SCHLEGEL .................................................................................. 1

**Special Section: Issues in the History and Memory of the OUN II**

Introduction: Essays in the Historical Interpretation of the Organization of Ukrainian Nationalists
ANDREAS UMLAND and YULIYA YURCHUK ......................................... 29

Catalytic Mobilization of Radical Ukrainian Nationalists in the Second Polish Republic:
The Impact of Political Opportunity Structure
IVAN GOMZA ........................................................................................ 35

Allies or Collaborators? The Organization of Ukrainian Nationalists and Nazi Germany during the Occupation of Ukraine in 1941–43
IGOR BARINOV ..................................................................................... 77

Volodymyr Viatrovych's *Second Polish–Ukrainian War*
MYROSLAV SHKANDRIJ ...................................................................... 105

**Correspondence**

JOHN-PAUL HIMKA ............................................................................. 131

**Reviews**

Christoph Mick, *Lemberg, Lwów, L'viv, 1914–1947: Violence and Ethnicity in a Contested City*
SERHY YEKELCHYK .............................................................................. 133

Tarik Cyril Amar, *The Paradox of Ukrainian Lviv:*
*A Borderland City between Stalinists, Nazis, and Nationalists*
Yulia Oreshina .................................................................................. 135

Victoria Khiterer, *Jewish Pogroms in Kiev during*
*the Russian Civil War, 1918–1920*
Christopher Gilley ....................................................................... 138

Leonid Rein, *The Kings and the Pawns: Collaboration*
*in Byelorussia during World War II*
Anika Walke ................................................................................... 142

Andrea Graziosi and Frank E. Sysyn (eds.), *Communism*
*and Hunger: the Ukrainian, Kazakh and Soviet Famines*
*in Comparative Perspective*
Karolina Koziura ......................................................................... 146

Mikhail Minakov, *Development and Dystopia:*
*Studies in Post-Soviet Ukraine and Eastern Europe*
Maryna Rabinovych ........................................................................ 149

Sander Brouwer (ed.), *Contested Interpretations of the Past in*
*Polish, Russian, and Ukrainian Film: Screen as Battlefield*
Olga Gontarska .............................................................................. 153

Shaun Walker, *The Long Hangover: Putin's New Russia*
*and the Ghosts of the Past*
Antony Kalashnikov ........................................................................ 156


About the Contributors ................................................................ 161

# Soviet Bureaucracy as a Category Coining Machine: Ethnicity, Ethnography, and the "Primordial Trap"

Simon Schlegel[*]

*Abstract:* *Soviet use of ethnicity as an administrative category significantly changed the way ethnic groups and the boundaries between them came to be conceived. The ascription of ethnic identities through the Soviet passport system is very well studied. It is less clear, however, how this practice was justified when faced with contradiction and how the theoretical concepts behind it became common and lasting beliefs. In a long-term assessment of the consequences of Soviet administrative practices, this study combines archival research and biographical interviews to uncover the deep imprints Soviet ethnicity policies left on contemporary forms of categorization. Research was conducted in southern Bessarabia, a multi-ethnic and peripheral region of south-western Ukraine. Through this local lens, the study takes a close look at how Soviet social sciences dealt with contradictions that occurred between its clear-cut categories and a fuzzier social reality. The paper shows that the main strategy to overcome such ambiguity has been to coin new social categories whenever the established ones failed to accommodate all observable cases. I argue that this solution leads into a "primordial trap," the claim that all these newly coined categories had existed long before anyone realized. Soviet institutions combined three practices that led ethnicity to be taken as a natural and decisive part of everyone's identity: Soviet social sciences declared ethnicity an essential category; the Soviet education apparatus made ethnicity a pervasive reality; and Soviet*

---

[*] The author wishes to thank the Max Planck Institute for Social Anthropology in Halle (Saale), Germany, for its generous funding of the research on which this paper is based.

*administration ascribed one ethnic label to each of its citizens. Retracing these three practices, the article examines the underlying scholarly theories and the resulting folk theories which tend to lead into the "primordial trap." The state that created today's dominant ethnicity concepts may have long vanished, but the inbuilt evasive maneuver of creating ever new categories on the blurred boundaries of obsolete ones made its ethnicity concepts remarkably resilient.*

This study examines how the Soviet usage of ethnicity as an administrative category shaped the way ethnicity is used by state actors and among the wider public of post-soviet Ukraine. The argument focuses on three main practices; the coining of ethnic categories by administrators and scholars, the dissemination of these categories through the state's educational and cultural institutions, and the ascription of these categories to individual citizens. The study is based on fieldwork between September 2012 and December 2013 in a peripheral and ethnically very diverse region of south-western Ukraine, a region most commonly referred to as southern Bessarabia. Today, this region is largely Russian speaking.[1] In the main town, Izmail, Russians and Ukrainians together amount to roughly 80 per cent of the population. Many of the villages in the town's vicinity are inhabited predominantly by Bulgarians, Moldovans, or the Turkic speaking Gagauz. The Gagauz, like their neighbors, are mainly Orthodox Christians. Together with Bulgarians and a much smaller group of Albanians, they came to this Region as agricultural settlers from the territory of modern-day Bulgaria, mainly around the year of 1812, when the Ottoman Empire had to cede Bessarabia to Russia (Kushko and Taki 2012: 164). Based on an approach that blends methods from history and anthropology, this article looks for

---

[1] This means that in public situations, most people would start a conversation with a stranger in Russian. The latest all-Ukrainian census from 2001 indicates for Odessa oblast' a slight majority of people who call Ukrainian their native language (46.3%) over Russian (41.9%) (http://2001.ukrcensus.gov.ua/regions/reg_odes/), but also a slight majority of people who say Russian is the language they are most fluent in (http://2001.ukrcensus.gov.ua/results/nationality_population/graphic#m4). Unless indicated otherwise, all URLs provided in this article were last accessed on 30 September 2018.

traces of the past in the present by asking people questions about their past and by analyzing archived administrative documents[2] in order to unearth state practices that are no longer directly observable. The Soviet state's usage of the social category "ethnicity" (called "natsional'nost'" in bureaucracy but "ethnos" in social sciences) created boundaries between people. These boundaries have lately changed their functions, but have lost none of their significance. How have they been maintained for so long, even after the bureaucracy that originally created them has gone? The following case study of inclusion and exclusion can help to find answers by reconstructing the history of local ideas about ethnicity.

## Making Ethnicity an Objectively Ascribable Category

When speaking about Soviet administration, we need to carefully discern between an old seventy-year zone and a younger forty-year zone (Gellner 1990: 283). When the Union expanded beyond its original post-Civil-War borders into western Ukraine in 1939 and into the Baltic states and Bessarabia in 1940, it already had nearly two decades of experience using ethnicity as a bureaucratic category (Martin 2001; Slezkine 1994; Suny 2001). To use ethnicity effectively for administrative purposes, it needed to be molded into an unambiguously ascribable category, very much like more familiar bureaucratic categories such as age or tax class. To achieve this goal, Soviet bureaucracy heavily relied on a fitting set of theories provided by the social sciences, especially ethnography. Of interest here are the mechanisms triggered when these theories ran into contradiction and needed readjustment. In order to put the coining of categories into a perspective that will allow us to better comprehend the resulting bureaucratic practices, I argue that all usages of ethnicity as an objectively ascribable category are imperiled to get stuck in a

---

[2] Archival sources used in this research come from the state archive in Izmail. It is a branch (*filial*) of the state archive in the provincial capital Odessa, which is directly subordinated to the head of the oblast' administration. The archive's full name is Komunal'na ustanova "Izmail'skyi arkhiv" (Communal organization "Archive of Izmail"). In the archival references in this article, "Fr" indicates collections from the Soviet period.

"primordial trap." This is the term I use to describe a theoretical dead-end into which Soviet ethnicity theories led against their declared intention. If Soviet social sciences had been pluralistic and free, then someone would have eventually thought of a way to avoid this trap. But because Soviet social sciences were a captive of the one-party state, as Tishkov (1992, 1997) convincingly points out, scholars had no choice but to sugarcoat their theories' path to the "primordial trap."

In Soviet ethnography each ethnic group was portrayed as a learning organism during the long evolutionary process that culminates in communism, and each group was conceptualized to have developed a distinct character that made it unique in the community of Soviet peoples (Bromley and Podol'niy 1990: 106; Shnirelman 2009: 114). Theories stipulating unique ethnic characteristics that stuck to every person justified registering ethnicity in a person's passport. They also facilitated the question how to approach ethnic diversity. Members of one ethnic group appeared to be united by a common origin and led by one motivation (Solonari 2003: 418). If one ethnic group was deemed, for instance, unreliable, then everyone whose personal documents contained this ascription could be treated in exactly the same way. The Soviet Union's centrally planning administration would have been infinitely more complex if state authorities had to check whether each individual in fact exhibited a particular character or not. The proxy of ethnicity for reliability and other characteristics dramatically reduced decision-making complexity. The bureaucratic practice of categorization by ethnicity may not have made Soviet administration fairer, but it certainly made it easier and cheaper.

The metaphor of a "trap" is appropriate for the underlying theories, because no Soviet theory intentionally claimed ethnicity was primordial or essential. One indication that there was no such intention is that Soviet ethnicity theories heavily relied on the concept of *ethnogenesis*. To describe this process, Soviet ethnographers closely collaborated with archaeologists and linguists. In this way, they hoped to trace the origins, the evolution, and in some cases the disappearance of entities called "ethnos" (Bromley 1980: 160; Shnirelman 2009: 114). For many ethnic groups, Soviet social sciences provided elaborate histories and precise indications as to at which point in time this particular group came into being. Soviet ethnography did not therefore claim that ethnic groups had existed since times immemorial, or that they were immune to change. Yet one of the main purposes of studying ethnogenesis was to determine a group's developmental stage and to ascribe a fitting hierarchical status such as "ethnos" or "sub-ethnos" to each delimited group (Tishkov 1992: 373). This status then could be significant for the standing of the people who were registered as members of that group. Meanwhile in the West, social scientists such as Anderson (2006), Gellner (1983), and Hobsbawm and Ranger (1983) began deconstructing the category of ethnicity, by retracing the history of the category's construction. The Soviet Union, however, built part of its power on these categories. Had ethnography started to deconstruct these categories, it would have put the discipline at odds with party elites. Therefore, Soviet social sciences secluded itself behind an iron curtain of terminology and continued working with concepts of ethnicity that could not be deconstructed because they occurred naturally and were held together by a naturally occurring essence. Soviet theories never explicitly named this essence, but implicitly assumed one.

The use of ethnicity as an administrative category allowed the administration to treat people of the same ethnicity the same and people of different ethnicities in different ways. Justification for unequal treatment of different groups only holds if the alleged differences in character are congruent with ascribed ethnic categories. This is why Soviet ethnicity theories came along with a strong, however unvoiced, reservation against the blending of ethnic groups and the dissolution of ethnic boundaries. This process would remain reserved for a future post-ethnic age in which a unified Soviet People would absorb all earlier categories. But for the present, Soviet ethnographers believed they should best describe undiluted ethnic groups. Field sites for ethnographic studies were, among other factors, selected by the criterion of cultural homogeneity and typicality (Haber 2014: 209).

There was an equally strong distaste for the idea that people individually chose their ethnicity from a menu of possible ethnic identities. Bureaucratic categories are normally introduced so that people with certain givens can be treated in certain ways. Most such categories are not for choice, because state policies towards certain subjects are meant to manipulate these subjects, they are not meant to *be manipulated by the subjects*. This is why, in any bureaucratic system, people are typically not allowed to choose their age, gender, or tax class. By using ethnicity as a bureaucratic category, it was implicitly also conceived as a category which people should not be allowed to choose or change themselves. Of course, in reality, people did change their ethnic affiliation (see Gorenburg 1999, 2006 for case studies), but unlike for other categories, such as party membership or citizenship, the state did not control or define the procedure involved in this identity change. Because the Soviets introduced their own list of possible ethnic belongings, many people, upon first ascription, did have to choose what ethnic group they belonged to (or fall back on to a choice made by a representative of the preceding Romanian bureaucracy). The Soviet theory assumed that in most cases this would be an unambiguous decision and that if it was not, a local expert would be able to give objective reasons why one ethnic identity rather than another should be ascribed. (In rare cases local clerks changed an ethnic identity as chosen by people or Romanian administrators, because they decided it was a mistaken choice).[3] The whole point was that after having been ascribed an allegedly objective category, people should not be able to change it any more.

Most post-Soviet countries have erased the category of ethnicity from identity documents of their citizens. In Ukraine the "fifth line" (*piataia grafa*) of the passport, the line that specified ethnicity, was abolished in 1995. But politicians who want to reserve special

---

[3] A scholar from Chișinău showed me the marriage documents of his grandparents who married in 1950 near Kotovsk (now Podols'k), a small town in the north of Odessa oblast'. The village where they lived was in the Ukrainian SSR but very close to the border with the Moldovan SSR. On the couple's birth certificates that had been issued on the basis of Romanian documents, the fifth line had been manipulated on the occasion of the wedding. The word "Moldovan" was crossed out and the word "Ukrainian" was added in handwriting. A handwritten instruction on the flipside of the documents read: "change of ethnicity valid, trust!"

rights for specific ethnic groups have recently expressed their nostalgia for it.[4]

The boundaries that continue to shape local politics in independent Ukraine have their roots in the Soviet state's preference for grand-scheme planning. Clear-cut categories were indispensable for a society engineered to fulfill centrally planned outcomes. Therefore, one scholarly priority for leading Soviet theoreticians was the production and dissemination of new categories. Each newly coined category gave the discipline a claim to better understand society and to be able to offer more finely tuned planning solutions. James Scott's concept of "legibility" fits this observation very well. Because most states are much younger than the societies they administer, they need to introduce categories that enable them to "read" and eventually manipulate society (Scott 1998: 183). Programmatic thinkers in Soviet ethnography saw the discipline as an auxiliary data-generating machine to social engineering. Sergey Tokarew argued the Soviet state had turned ethnography from a discipline of lay enthusiasts to a matter of national interest (Tokarew 1954: 9). As an example of ethnography's practical applicability, Pavel Kushner (1951: 18–19) suggested that ethnicity statistics be used in order to draw administrative borders more precisely and to develop school curricula according to the specific needs of each group. Another direct application of ethnographic knowledge he saw in the transformation of Soviet peasant households from units of production to units of consumption (Kushner 1974: 196–97). But most markedly, Soviet scholars of ethnicity catered to the state's need for "legibility" by introducing hierarchically ordered categories of ethnic groups such as "super-ethnos," "ethnos," "sub-ethnos," "ethnikos," and "ethnographic group," that were used along with other categories such

---

[4] In 2009, Vladimir Litvin, then the speaker of the Ukrainian Parliament, was cited saying "I want the fifth line to be reintroduced. We need it, so we know who our forefathers were. Why would anyone be ashamed of that?"; *Ukrainskaia Pravda*, 24 April 2009, http://www.pravda.com.ua/rus/news/2009/04/24/4482170/. The far-right Svoboda party demands the reintroduction of a person's ethnicity in identity documents high up in their party program; See item 1.11 in Svoboda's party program) at https://svoboda.org.ua/wp-content/uploads/2018/08/PZU_actual_text_1-44.pdf.

as "population" and "race" (a category that was itself split into three main subgroups, which contained twenty smaller groups, which then branched into different "anthropological types"). All these categories were carefully defined by a list of characteristics (Bromley 1983: 14–43). This social dimension of category building was paired by similarly bounded temporal categories such as the development stages "archaic," "slavery," "feudalism," "capitalism," and "socialism" (*ibid.:* 36). Together, these categories laid a grid plan of social theory over time and space. Each group somewhere fitted into this grid. Each box in the grid plan could be addressed with a specific set of policies, a tailor-made social engineering program.

Soviet scholars like Mikhail Sergeyev, an expert on the "small nations of the North," strongly advocated a specific policy for each ethnic group in its particular environment. Giving ethnic groups living under different circumstances various forms of political self-determination would "facilitate the organization and activization of backward peoples" (Sergeyev 1964: 488). Without the "legibility" created by social and historical categories, the sheer complexity of administering a huge and diverse country towards very ambitious goals would have been overwhelming. The problem in Soviet administration was not the creation and use of categories (no state can do without). The problem rather was the low degree of critical reflection upon these categories. In a state where criticism of official theories was punished, the theoretical model was increasingly taken for reality (Scott 1998: 196). This becomes even more clear after considering the argument of Skalnik that the dominant paradigm of Soviet ethnography was circular: *Etnografiia* was defined as the study of ethnos, and ethnos was defined as the subject of *etnografiia* (Skalnik 1990: 148). If, in this roundabout, reality did not fit the theory, a new sub-category could be introduced until all ethnic groups somehow fit into the Soviet Union's grid plan. For groups which claimed a similar status for themselves but did not fulfill the list of criteria set by the rule book, new categories substituted a discussion about the validity of established categories. The terms "ethnographic group" and "sub-ethnos" could serve this purpose. They were introduced to designate groups that were found to be culturally different from an established ethnic category, but where it was inconvenient to establish a separate political approach.⁵ Instead of revisiting established categories, social scientists created a new category for each case that did not fit. Soviet social sciences thereby became a category coining machine. The mindset that ethnic groups were self-contained and inherently different from each other became inside the Soviet Union what Thomas Kuhn called a "paradigm," that is a set of "universally recognized scientific achievements that for a time provide model problems and solutions to a community of practitioners" (Kuhn 1996: x). The unease with the paradigm of his time is manifest in Bromley's writings. Especially when he wrote to convince western audiences of his theory, every definition is followed by a relativization, every category is first demarcated, then its demarcations are softened. For example, Bromley introduces his definition of "ethnos" just to say that a lot more research will be needed to grasp the full complexity of this form of human society. Or he discusses several subcategories of "race" and treats them as analytical categories, just to add that none of them have clear boundaries (Bromley 1980). Leading theoreticians around Bromley understood the pitfalls of essentializing ethnicity and they denied believing in an essential quality that was innate to all members of one "ethnos" (Bromley and Podol'nii 1990: 106). Yet the paradigm in which their discipline was embedded did not leave room for an overhaul of the entire ethnicity concept. The need for clear-cut categories in a centrally planning administration led to an academic preference for supposedly objective realities. Whenever this objectivity was challenged, Soviet scholars hurriedly invented new, allegedly clear-cut categories, and thereby renewed the claim that they found something that had already been there independent of observation and long before anyone realized. It is this reoccurring mechanism that lets the primordial trap snap shut. Nobody intended to claim primordially existing groups, yet implicitly Soviet ethnographers did so

---

5    In Carpathian Ukraine the groups Boyko, Lemkos, and Hutsuls were sometimes described as "ethnographic groups," thereby acknowledging their cultural distinctness but denying them the status of a fully sovereign "ethnos" (Makarchuk 2008: 19). In Russia the Don Cossacks or the Pomori of the White Sea coast have been described as "sub-ethnos" of the Russian ethnos (Bromley and Podol'nii 1984: 19).

every time they drew new boundaries between newly discovered categories of people. This system led into a trap, but it also prevented Soviet ethnography's basic categories from dissolving, at least as long as the discipline was tightly controlled and isolated.

Kuhn observed that revolutionizing a whole paradigm could only commence once its failure was obvious. Without a deep crisis in the established paradigm there are hardly enough incentives to discard it and develop a new one (Kuhn 1996: 76–78). The flaws in the established paradigm might have been obvious to many practitioners of the discipline, but in the Soviet Union it was only one of many conspicuous flaws that awaited reform. As long as a paradigm shift could be avoided, scholars would modify their theories by adding ever new sub-categories to circumvent any apparent conflict. The primordial trap was quietly accepted as a side effect.

## Making Ethnicity a "Pervasive Reality"

To turn this theoretical dead end into a train of thought that eventually was taken for granted was the result of an impressive didactic campaign. Although this campaign was relatively short, it left a lasting impact. It started after World War II, and passed its zenith during the Brezhnev years. The Soviet state that orchestrated this campaign had no incentive to disseminate concepts of ethnicity that would challenge its policies towards ethnic minorities or its bureaucratic practices. As a consequence, the state's bureaucratic categories soon became "pervasive realities" (Karklins 1986: 43). How could a theory be turned into a reality so quickly? What made this theory so convincing to so many people? Is the answer to be found in the theory itself or in the social relations that brought this theory to the people? Social scientists need to deal at least with two sorts of theories: the theories of the people they study, the "folk theory," and the theory they analyze their subjects' theories with, "analytical theory" (Burawoy 2009: 270). When we study ethnicity concepts in the former Soviet Union we need to study a third strand of theory, the analytical theory of the defunct Soviet system around the framework of which "folk theory" is still recognizably built. Analytical theories either deconstruct folk theory or build on it. The Soviet ethnographers whose work I discuss here did neither of the two. They were an auxiliary force in a social engineering campaign tasked with creating an acceptable justification for the problems the state's ethnicity policies created. Adding to the durability of their ideas is the fact that the education systems of the Soviet Union's successor states were not nearly as powerful as that of the Soviet Union. It is therefore no wonder that concepts of ethnicity, disseminated in the post-war decades, remained almost unchallenged by the education system of most post-Soviet states, including Ukraine's.

Even though, by the 1960s, ethnic differences had relatively little relevance for a person's standing within Soviet society, the category of ethnicity was constantly present, be it in public discourse on the village level or in wider society. In Ukraine, most people by that time had a passport, in the "fifth line" of which, their ethnic identity was registered. One way of turning newly introduced social categories into pervasive realities was attaching them to public figures. Once somebody started to engage in a public function, the social categories attached to them, became public knowledge. For instance, in village elections the hand-picked candidates were introduced to the public by a couple of basic characteristics. Ethnicity came right after name and age. Further information revealed the candidates' level of education, military or academic rank, place of work, and whether or not a candidate was a member or an aspired member of the party.[6] Putting ethnicity in a row with easily verifiable categories such as place of work and academic degree, suggested it was similarly straightforward. Ethnicity might no longer have hindered one group or the other from access to political power, but it was a constantly present category. Even in a much wider discourse, ethnicity had a stable place in the public sphere. Take for example the official congratulations to the cosmonaut German Titov for his achievement of the first ever completed 24-hour space flight in 1961. On the front page of Soviet newspapers, including local editions of *Pravda*, Titov was introduced to the Soviet public through the

---

[6] As indicated in the documentation of village elections for the village of Kotlovina in Reni rayon, one of the main field sites in this study; Izmail'skyi arkhiv, Fr. 367, d. 95 (Protokoly sobranii o kandidatov v deputaty sel'soveta).

following characteristics: "Comrade Titov German Stepanovich, born 1935, ethnicity: Russian, candidate party member since April 1961."[7] Ranking ethnicity so high up in the list of a person's characteristics has helped to produce a perception of ethnicity as an unchangeable, tangible, and unambiguously detectable human characteristic. Terry Martin (2000: 168) called it a "constant routine of ethnic labeling" that "inadvertently indoctrinated the Soviet population in the belief that ethnicity was an inherent, fundamental, and crucially important characteristic of all individuals."

For all that, Soviet officials made it clear early on that no ethnic group in Bessarabia was superior to any other. Certainly, the public insistence that all ethnic groups were equal and that they all deeply respected each other, still allowed discrimination on a subtler level. But publicly, ethnic diversity became a cause for celebration. In ethnically diverse regions, such as southern Bessarabia, celebrating multi-ethnicity became a lasting tradition that began with the advent of Soviet rule. Even today, hardly a political speech fails to mention how ethnically diverse Bessarabians are and how well they nevertheless get along. This recurring theme implicitly also suggests that it is an achievement to maintain peaceful inter-ethnic relations, because according to expectations, ethnic differences should routinely lead to conflict. The Soviet state claimed to include representatives of all ethnic groups in the decision-making processes and therefore to provide a political order that would prevent such conflict. Announcing elections for people's courts, in January 1949, the local party paper declared:

> In these [electoral] lists appear people of various ages and professions, Russians and Ukrainians, Bulgarians and Moldovans, members of the party and unaffiliated [candidates]. They are all united by a boundless love for the fatherland, by their devotion to the great cause of Lenin-Stalin, the cause of communism.[8]

With time, the fact that several ethnic groups lived peacefully together in Bessarabia became the single most important feature for

---

[7] *Pridunaiskaia Pravda*, Izmail, 10 August 1961, 1.
[8] *Pridunaiskaia Pravda*, Izmail, 8 January 1949, 1.

the region's representation. In the seminal reference book *The History of Towns and Villages of the Ukrainian SSR,* the section about southern Bessarabia began with the note that it was a multi-ethnic, but nevertheless very peaceful region.[9]

Since inter-ethnic harmony was seen as an achievement, it had to be earned by a collective effort, an effort centrally planned and organized by the party. In Bessarabia, this effort manifested itself as a pedagogical campaign. In schools and culture houses people from all walks of life were instructed in the Soviet perspective on history. These classes aimed not only at the liquidation of illiteracy but also of what was seen by Soviet administrators as rural backwardness. In the second half of the 1940s, the Izmail bureau of lecturers started an evening school program in surrounding villages, with lectures in Russian and Ukrainian.[10] Villagers were gathered to learn about topics as diverse as *Was there a beginning of the earth and will there be an end?, The natural resources of the Ukrainian SSR, How did life occur on earth?, Charles Darwin and his teachings,* or *The Stalinist constitution, the most democratic constitution in the world.*[11] In this canon of political education, many lessons were meant to attune village audiences to ethnicity as a household category, but also to convince them of what they probably already knew; that living in a multi-ethnic society was nothing bad. Ethnicity was always presented in combination with the Soviet catchphrase "friendship of peoples" (*druzhba narodov*). One standard lecture was *The Leninist-Stalinist friendship of peoples.*[12] In the lesson *The Soviet state, a state of a new and higher order,* villagers were told that:

> The Soviet state is the model of a multi-ethnic state. The multi-ethnic state is based on equal rights and the friendship of peoples. The Soviet state is the organizer of friendship between peoples, of mutual assistance between

---

[9]   *Istoriia gorodov i sel Ukrainskoi SSR – Odesskaia Oblast'* (Kyiv: Institut akademii nauk USSR, 1978).
[10]  Izmail'skyi arkhiv, Fr. 415, d. 10 (Temy lektsii dlia sel'skikh i kolkhoznykh klubov na 1947 god), ll. 19–21.
[11]  Ibid., d. 15 (Plany lektsii po istorii i literature), ll. 1–7.
[12]  Ibid., l. 10.

peoples, the organizer of equal rights for these peoples, and their moral and political unity.[13]

From lectures like these it became clear that ethnicity was real and had to be organized. Inter-ethnic relations, in order to be peaceful and friendly, had to be managed by a patronizing state. This state fostered the friendship between collective entities of ethnic groups by tasking translators, folklore groups, and ethnographic museums with providing the necessary intercultural contact to befriend one people with another (Slezkine 1994: 447). In Bessarabian villages the Soviet state appeared in the guise of the Ukrainian SSR. Accordingly, one set of talks dealt with the Ukrainian people, for instance *The emergence of the Ukrainian people* or *The development of a socialist Ukrainian culture*.[14] But lectures also took a fierce stand against Ukrainian aspirations of independence and against ethnic nationalism: the lecture curriculum of 1947 offered *Ukrainian bourgeois nationalism, the worst enemy of the Ukrainian people*, as well as *The struggle of Lenin and Stalin against bourgeois Ukrainian nationalism*, and *The destruction of the bourgeois nationalist counterrevolution during the Civil War*.[15] The fact that the words "bourgeois" and "nationalism" appeared exclusively in combination, will have made it clear to even the most illiterate *kolkhoznik* that ethnicity was only good as in "friendship of the peoples." True, there was one friendship that was more important than others, the one with the Russian people, the *outstanding nation and leading force of the Soviet Union*, as one lecture was titled.[16] The lecturers delivering these centrally planned presentations said nothing about the Bulgarians, Gagauz, or Albanians, let alone speaking to these groups in their respective languages. But the celebration of a multi-ethnic society, which became a self-congratulatory trade mark of Soviet public discourse, was certainly a well-meant attempt to give a sense of belonging even to these peripheral minorities.

---

[13] Ibid., d. 22 (Metodicheskie razrabotki v pomoshch' lektoram), l. 50.
[14] Ibid. d. 15, l. 14.
[15] Ibid., ll. 10, 14.
[16] Ibid., l. 12.

Although the rural ethnic minorities in southern Bessarabia had to learn Russian in order to access Soviet society, none of the Soviet campaigners or educators, who came to lecture them, suggested that they become Russians. Cultural differences, as long as they could be condensed into differing folkloric performances on the stages of culture houses, were cherished and the conservation of such differences was portrayed as an indicator of a group's resilience.[17] In the Soviet discourse, it was the elimination of class differences, not of ethnic differences, that was portrayed as the path to a prosperous and harmonious society. Once this was accomplished, nothing could be in the way of the "friendship of peoples."

Because the Soviet Union was almost a quarter of a century old when it took over Bessarabia, there had already been ample time to experiment with history curricula for mass education. The Central Committee of the Communist Party dealt with the issue in spring 1934. The commission for new textbooks and the Central Committee followed Stalin in appealing to history teachers to abjure "abstract sociological schemes" for a "chronological historical sequence in the exposition of historical events," and to emphasize "important events, personages, and dates" (Banerji 2006: 828; Karlsson 1993: 215). According to these directives, ethnicity was not treated as a phenomenon that occurred at a specific period in time and in response to specific needs. Instead, ethnic groups themselves were portrayed as historical personages that took part in historic events.

All states in the former Soviet Union carry the name of the ethnic majority group, the "titular nation" (*titul'naia natsiia*). This invites a metaphor in which the state, as something tangible and perceptible, stands for the more abstract concept of ethnicity. States comprise the territory of and provide the political guidance for the titular ethnic group. Also, states are acting entities. They arrange treaties with other states, they engage in trade and warfare, they can close or open their borders. Similarly, ethnic groups are often

---

[17] In an early Soviet folklore festival in 1953, the performance of traditional Bulgarian songs and dances was hailed by the party newspaper as a sign that their culture withstood the pressure of the "Romanian Boyar occupation"; "Rastsvetaiut narodnye talanty Izmail'shchiny," *Pridunaiskaia Pravda*, 28 November 1953.

portrayed as clearly bounded and steerable entities. Most prominently, the idea of ethnic groups as clearly bounded entities with a unique essence and as actors of history was coined by Yulian Bromley (1983), who served as the director of the ethnographic department of the Soviet Academy of Sciences from 1966–89. His theories matched a historical narrative in which ethnic groups come into contact with other groups of the same category, subjugate them or assimilate to them, move from one place to another, take on new lifestyles, faiths, and languages, fight for their independence and, ultimately, establish states of their own. Using the state as a metaphor for the ethnic group helps imagining the ethnic group as clearcut. The state after all is bounded by clearly demarcated borders. Dividing lines between states are a very common phenomenon, especially in places like southern Bessarabia, where people live in their proximity. State borders are guarded and present an obstacle. This feature often seems to be taken as self-evident for ethnic boundaries too. Although they rarely restrict people in their day-to-day activities, they are imagined as a dividing line that somehow must present an obstacle. They cannot simply be trespassed without justification. The state was not just instrumental in ascribing an ethnic category to everyone and turning ethnicity into a pervasive reality. The state, with its capacity to act and with its clear borders, also served as a metaphor for the conceptualization of ethnic groups: Just as states can be on friendly terms with one another, ethnic groups can live in a state of "friendship of peoples."

But if states and ethnic groups can live in friendship, primordial hostility is possible as well. In the history of southern Bessarabia, animosities with Germany and Romania took a prominent place in the Soviet pedagogical campaign. In lectures conducted by the Izmail lecturer bureau in the late 1940s, the historical perspective on this conflict reached right back to the Middle Ages: *The annihilation of the German-Swedish Occupants in the 12$^{th}$ and 13$^{th}$ century by Alexander Nevskii*, *The German aggression in the Middle Ages and the struggle against it*, and *The centuries long struggle of the Slavs against German occupants*.[18] In a lecture series, created especially for

---

[18] Izmail'skyi arkhiv, Fr. 415, d. 15, ll. 11–14.

Izmail *oblast'*, the Romanians, who had been driven out just years before, figured as prominent enemies. One approach to establish trust in the new Soviet government was a comparison with the Romanian regime of the interwar period: *How were elections conducted under the rule of the Romanian Boyars, and how are they conducted now?*[19] *The exposure of the reactionary and fascist ideologies of Romanian parties in Izmail region.*[20]

The hostility to these states clearly referred to a tangible experience in Soviet Bessarabia that the borders delimiting one's own country from these hostile outside forces provided protection. Whether state borders mark the line between hostile or friendly states, their relationship can only be reproduced if the border remains a clear-cut dividing line. Through its metaphorical translation, the same was true for ethnic boundaries: that ethnic groups in Bessarabia and in the rest of the Soviet Union lived together in "friendship of the peoples" did not—and still does not—mean that the boundaries between them lost their significance. Ethnicity could only remain a "pervasive reality" if the boundaries between ethnic groups were real and if a person could be either on one or the other side of such a boundary.

## Ascribing One (and Only One) Ethnic Identity to Everyone

The Soviet state established its reign in southern Bessarabia in the second half of the 1940s mainly by replacing village elites. The first cohort of administrators, Kolkhoz bosses, agronomists, doctors, veterinaries, and teachers, came from the old Soviet Union. They replaced a Romanian administration that had already paid very close attention to ethnicity. In the Romanian case, "legibility" of the ethnic situation served as the basis for policies meant to foster Romanians in the region and to side-line all those not considered Romanian enough to play a role in politics or the economy (Hausleitner 2004; Livezeanu 1995: 298–300). In contrast, the new Soviet elites claimed to create "legibility" for affirmative action on ethnic

---

[19] *Ibid.*, d. 10, l. 17.
[20] *Ibid.*, d. 15, l. 25.

minorities, the basis for managing ethnic diversity and creating the friendship of peoples. The Soviet state, with its already time-tested ethnicity policies, established itself in Bessarabian villages as a group of experts, able to reform every aspect of society. One of the first administrative measures they performed was ascribing ethnic identities to every one of their new subjects, along with other newly introduced categories: social background, party membership, and military and academic ranks.

Soviet passports were introduced in southern Bessarabia in 1956 (Boneva 2006: 53). But the ethnicity criterion was used in registries long before. Counter to the state's claim of non-discrimination, belonging to an ethnic minority, especially during and after World War II, could mean profiting from collective ethnic rights or suffering from collective ethnic punishment. Therefore, in certain situations, very tangible and serious aspects of an individual biography could depend on one's belonging to an ethnic category. The most prominent historical example in the case of Bessarabia was the so-called "labor front," a euphemism for forced labor during World War II, which affected mainly people who were seen as representatives of enemy nations, such as Germans, Finns, Hungarians, and Bulgarians.[21] When, with Romanian and German troops retreating, Bessarabia came under firm Soviet control in late August 1944, lists of all men in the newly acquired provinces were quickly produced. They served as the basis for conscription. Although the war against Germany at that time was far from over, not all able-bodied men were recruited to fight at the front. Some were sent to toil in mines and smokestack industries in the Urals, the Donbas, Siberia, and Kazakhstan. The criterion by which a man was sent either west to fight on the front or east to work on the labor front, was ethnicity. Most men whose ethnicity was registered as Gagauz or as Bulgarian were sent to the labor front (Grek and Russev 2011: 98). Most men whose

---

[21] Lexikon der Vertreibungen - Deportation, Zwangsaussiedlung und ethnische Säuberung im Europa des 20. Jahrhunderts (Brandes *et al.* 2010: 41–44, 281). The term used in Bessarabia by my informants was not *trudarmiia*, but *trudovoi front*, "labor front."

ethnicity was Russian, Ukrainian, or Moldovan were recruited into the Red Army.[22]

Officially, such crucial decisions were a matter of objective fact checking. The citizen's ethnicity was ascribed based on the ethnicity of his or her parents (Ahlberg 1991: 806). Census findings about ethnicity relied largely on ethnic self-identification (Gorenburg 2006: 295). In practice, however, the choice was very restricted to a short, state-defined list of options. This list offered only clear-cut categories with no grey-zones between them. Ascription of ethnic categories therefore, in most cases, meant census takers, who suggested a selection of unambiguous categories to the people they registered to decide for. This required people to make a choice that they never had to make before in such clarity. In ethnically diverse regions like southern Bessarabia, this led to an interaction of citizens with the state that turned flexible and often blurred social categories into unambiguous administrative categories. The Soviets were not the first to struggle with such ambiguity. Their bureaucratic predecessors, the state servants of the Russian Empire, had already failed to come up with a reliable headcount revealing how many people of which ethnic category lived in the country. In 1897 the first and only empire-wide census took place in Russia (Cadiot 2005: 440). "The fiction of the census," as Anderson (2006: 166) observed, "is that everyone is in it and that everyone has one—and only one—extremely clear place," hence the census taker's "intolerance of multiple, politically 'transvestite', blurred, or changing identifications."

As Bessarabians left behind World War II, the ascription of ethnicity was increasingly used for affirmative purposes, mainly in education. School curricula and later clubs and culture house programs were tailor-made for the ethnic majority group in each village.

---

[22] Archived conscription lists from late 1944 confirm that when recruiting in Gagauz villages, Soviet recruiters produced separate lists for ethnic Gagauz men and for Russians; Izmail'skyi arkhiv, Fr. 367, d.5 (Spisok voennoobiazannykh po sel'skomu sovetu za 1944). Whereas the lists of Russian men reveal the army unit to which the conscripts were assigned, only interviews with four of the surviving men in summer 2013 could reveal that Gagauz men on the list were sent to the "labor front" in Cheliabinsk *oblast'*.

So if the administrative ascription of ethnicity was used to delimit the trustworthy from the suspicious in insecure times, in times of stability it was used to achieve the Soviet state's ambitious goals of providing education and economic growth. For some ethnic groups, ethnicity continued to be fateful, especially for Jews, whom the state increasingly saw as potential emigrants to Israel (Friedberg 1991: 10, 75). Ethnicity also remained problematic for ethnic groups that had been collectively accused and deported as traitors during World War II, such as the Chechens (Wanner 1998: 14) or the Crimean Tatars (Katchanovski 2005: 889).

Because of the state's aversion to changing an ethnic identity once it was ascribed, choosing an ethnic identity after the advent of Soviet power included many practical deliberations (Gorenburg 2006). The example of the labor front demonstrates that Soviet ethnicity ascriptions were by no means without consequence. And many of the people with the opportunity to choose, oriented their decision on those consequences. Interestingly, informants could hardly remember the actual procedure of bureaucratic ascription. Where, when, and under which circumstances their ethnicity was inscribed in identity documents had escaped the memory of most. What stuck in their minds were the explanations and justifications of those people with mixed ethnic ancestry, why they ended up being ascribed the ethnic identity their Soviet passports sported. Notably, for the first Soviet generation in southern Bessarabia, a particular ethnic belonging had to be justified, not proven. But except for the rare cases in which there were no question marks at all about someone's ethnic belonging, some sort of a justification was required. These explanations might be spatial ("I was living in a Gagauz village after all"); linguistic ("I speak Russian, don't I?"); kin-related ("everyone on my father's side of the family is Bulgarian"); related to an inner disposition ("I just feel that I belong to the Ukrainian Nation"); or to changes in one's biography ("after marriage I came into a Bulgarian family, and we spoke Bulgarian at home").

The need for such narratives marks a clear difference to the Romanians, who looked for what they thought was hard, factual proof of someone's ethnicity. Under their laws, access to state jobs, to education, and the military were reserved for ethnic Romanians (Hausleitner 2004; Livezeanu 1998). In the Romanian system, too much in terms of privilege and punishment depended on this ascription for it to be left merely to the justifying narratives of individual families. Such "hard proof" is again needed to acquire the citizenship rights and passports handed out by states in the historic homelands of Bessarabia's ethnic minorities. Petitioners willing to obtain a Bulgarian passport and the relative privileges that come with it need proof of Bulgarian ethnic ancestry. Such proof has to consist of documents demonstrating the Bulgarian ethnicity of the petitioner's ancestors, proving the petitioner's relation with these ancestors, as well as a formal declaration of Bulgarian self-identification.[23]

The Soviet state in contrast, upheld the claim that neither privilege nor punishment could be administered on the grounds of ethnicity. Therefore, the choice between different available ethnic identities would have had no consequences. The Soviet state could therefore confidently leave the justificatory narrative to its citizens and did not demand any more proof than the ethnic ascriptions made to earlier generations. This practice did not mean that in theory Soviet bureaucrats thought ethnicity was an obsolete category, or a category up to individual choice. But in contrast to the Soviet Union's predecessor and successor states, Soviet administrators needed to know about ethnicity first and foremost for legibility purposes rather than for the allocation of privilege or discrimination. All the more so, choices made for legibility purposes could not be picked from an open-ended list or a continuum that would dissolve the state-approved categories.

That justificatory narratives for ethnic choices survived the Soviet system and that newly independent states again ask for hard proof of ethnic belonging, suggests that the idea of clear-cut ethnic groups provided a bridge between state practices and folk theories. That academia has now been largely relieved from the uneasy role

---

[23] See instructions on the website of the *Dŭrzhavna agentsie za bŭlgarite v chuzhbina*, the state agency for Bulgarians living abroad; http://aba.government.bg/?legal=3.

of catering to the state, has not changed the appeal of ethnicity as an essential category for either the state or its citizens. In many cases, academia too continues to use the Soviet paradigm with its inbuilt mechanism to avoid contradiction. The Soviet category coining machine thereby remains productive long after its makers have left the stage.

## Conclusion

In order to render practicable the centrally planned administration of an ethnically diverse country, like the Soviet Union, a range of unambiguously ascribable bureaucratic categories were used. Even though social reality was often fuzzier, theories of ethnicity unintentionally assumed an essence that held this category together and clearly demarcated it from other groups of the same category. The resonance of this assumption can still be felt today in how ethnicity is conceptualized and performed in public. Soviet theories treated ethnic groups as actors of history and ascribed each of them a precise place in a comprehensive grid plan that allowed addressing each period and each territory with a specific policy. The more this model informed bureaucratic practices, the more it was taken for a social reality, a reality in which everyone has a clear place.

My findings from the archive show that when people in southern Bessarabia were instructed in history, this grid plan did not just serve as a theoretical model or a metaphor but as the structure of a grand narrative about the state and its subjects. This grand narrative was quickly adopted in myriad individual and family narratives that defined a person's place in society, in the Soviet state, and eventually in one (or several) of its successor states. The underlying analytical theory was quickly discarded after the disintegration of the Soviet Union (Sokolovskiy 2012; and most prominently by Tishkov 2003). Therefore, bureaucrats must now base their decisions about the ethnic identity of their clients on less formal sources than the passport. This leads them to demand what they consider hard proof of someone's ethnicity, unlike their Soviet predecessors, who claimed to use ethnic ascription only for legibility's sake, and no longer for the allocation of privilege or discrimination. But the grand narrative conveyed by Soviet educators lingers on as folk theory. Part of its resilience in the face of contradiction is that it entailed an inbuilt evasive maneuver. If the theory did not fit an observed case, it was not the theory that was adapted; rather, the categories encountered by ethnographers were constantly subdivided into ever smaller units in order to keep up the claim that the categories' boundaries were clear-cut and meaningful.

REFERENCES

Ahlberg, René. (1991) "Das sowjetische Paßsystem – ein Instrument bürokratischer Herrschaft," *Osteuropa* 8 (1991): 802–17.

Anderson, Benedict. (2006) *Imagined Communities: Reflections on the Origin and Spread of Nationalism (Revised Edition)*. London: Verso.

Banerji, Arup. (2006) "Notes on the Histories of History in the Soviet Union," *Economic & Political Weekly* 41(9): 826–33.

Boneva, Tanya. (2006) "Continuity and Identity in the Local Community: A Long-Term Perspective," *Anthropology of East Europe Review* 24(1): 51–58.

Brandes, Detlef, Sundhaussen, Holm, and Troebst, Stefan. (eds.) (2010) *Lexikon der Vertreibungen. Deportation, Zwangsaussiedlung und ethnische Säuberung im Europa des 20. Jahrhunderts*. Wien, Köln, Weimar: Böhlau.

Bromley, Yulian Vladimirovich. (1983) *Ocherki teorii etnosa*. Moskva: Nauka.

Bromley, Yulian Vladimirovich. (1980) "The Object and the Subject-Matter of Ethnography," in Ernest Gellner (ed.) *Soviet and Western Anthropology*. New York: Columbia University Press, 151–60.

Bromley, Yulian Vladimirovich, and Podol'nii, Roman Grigor'evich. (1990) *Chelovechestvo eto narody*. Moskva: Izdatel'stvo Mysl'.

Bromley, Yulian Vladimirovich, and Podol'nii Roman Grigor'evich. (1984) *Sozdano chelovechestvom*. Moskva: Politizdat.

Burawoy, Michael. (2009) *The Extended Case Method—Four Countries, Four Decades, Four Great Transformations, and One Theoretical Tradition*. Berkley, Los Angeles: University of California Press.

Cadiot, Juliette. (2005) "Searching for Nationality: Statistics and National Categories at the End of the Russian Empire (1897-1917)," *Russian Review* 64(3): 440–55.

Friedberg, Maurice. (1991) *How Things were done in Odessa: Cultural and Intellectual Pursuits in a Soviet City*. Oxford: Westview Press.

Gellner, Ernest. (1990) "Ethnicity and Faith in Eastern Europe," *Daedalus* 199(1): 279–94.

Gellner, Ernest. (1983) *Nations and Nationalism*. Ithaca: Cornell University Press.
Gorenburg, Dmitry. (2006) "Soviet Nationalities Policy and Assimilation," in Dominique Arel and Blair A. Ruble (eds.) *Rebounding Identities: The Politics of identities in Russia and Ukraine*. Baltimore: The John Hopkins University Press, 273-303.
Gorenburg, Dmitry. (1999) "Identity Change in Bashkortostan: Tatars into Bashkirs and Back," *Ethnic and Racial Studies* 22(3): 554-80.
Grek, I.F. and Russev, N.D. (2011) *1812 povorotnyi god v istorii Budzhaka i "zadunaiskikh pereselentsev."* Chişinău: Stratum Plus.
Haber, Maya. (2014) "The Soviet Ethnographers as a Social Engineer—Socialist Realism and the Study of Rural Life, 1945-1958," *The Soviet and Post-Soviet Review* 41 (2014): 194-219.
Hausleitner, Mariana. (2004) "Minderheitenpolitik in Grossrumänien zwischen 1918 und 1944," in Larisa Schippel (ed.) *Im Dialog: Rumänistik im deutschsprachigen Raum*. Frankfurt a.M: Peter Lang, 361-76.
Hobsbawm, Eric, and Ranger, Terence. (1983) *The Invention of Tradition*. Cambridge: Cambridge University Press.
Karklins, Rasma. (1986) *Ethnic Relations in the USSR, the Perspective from Below*. Boston: Unwin Hyman.
Karlsson, Klas-Göran. (1993) "History Teaching in Twentieth-century Russia and the Soviet Union: Classicism and its Alternatives," in Ben Eklof (ed.) *School and Society in Tsarist and Soviet Russia, Selected papers from the Fourth World Congress for Soviet and East European Studies*. New York: St. Martin's Press, 204-23.
Katchanovski, Ivan. (2005) "Small Nations but Great Differences: Political Orientations and Cultures of the Crimean Tatars and the Gagauz," *Europe-Asia Studies* 57(6): 877-94.
Kuhn, Thomas S. (1996) *The Structure of Scientific Revolutions*. Chicago and London: University of Chicago Press.
Kushko, Andrey, and Taki, Viktor (2012), *Bessarabiia v sostave Rossiiskoi imperii 1812-1917*. Moskva: Novoe Literaturnoe Obozrenie.
Kushner, Pavel Ivanovich. (1974) "On some Processes Taking Place in the Contemporary Kolkhoz Family," in Stephen Dunn, and Ethel Dunn (eds.) *Introduction into Soviet Ethnography Volume I*. Berkeley: Highgate Road Social Science Research Station, 195-213.
Kushner, Pavel Ivanovich. (1951) *Etnicheskie territorii i etnicheskie granitsy*. Moskva: Izdatel'stvo Akademii Nauk SSSR.
Livezeanu, Irina. (1998): "Interwar Poland and Romania: The Nationalization of Elites, the Vanishing Middle, and the Problem of Intellectuals," *Harvard Ukrainian Studies* 22 (1998): 407-30.

Livezeanu, Irina. (1995) *Cultural Politics in Greater Romania: Regionalism, Nation Building and Ethnic Struggle 1918-1930*. Ithaca: Cornell University Press.

Makarchuk, S. A. (2008) *Etnichna istoriia Ukrainy*. Kyiv: Znannia.

Martin, Terry. (2001) *The Affirmative Action Empire: Nations and Nationalism in the Soviet Union, 1923-1939*. Ithaca and London: Cornell University Press.

Martin, Terry. (2000) "Modernization or Neotraditionalism? Ascribed Nationality and Soviet Primordialism," in David L. Hoffmann and Yannis Kotsonis (eds.) *Russian Modernity: Politics, Knowledge, Practices*. New York: Macmillan Press, 161–84.

N. A. (1978) *Istoriia gorodov i sel Ukrainskoi SSR – Odesskaia Oblast'*, Kyiv: Institut Akademii Nauk USSR.

Scott, James C. (1998) *Seeing like a State: How Certain Schemes to Improve the Human Condition have Failed*. New Haven and London: Yale University Press.

Sergeyev, Mikhail Alekseevich. (1964) "The Building of Socialism among the Peoples of Northern Siberia and the Soviet Far East," in M.G. Levin and L.P. Potapov (eds.) *The Peoples of Siberia*. Chicago: The University of Chicago Press, 487–510.

Shnirelman, Victor. (2009) "Stigmatized by History or by Historians? The Peoples of Russia in School History Textbooks," *History and Memory* 21(2): 110–49.

Skalnik, Peter. (1990) "Soviet Etnografiia and the National(ities) Question," *Cahiers du Monde russe et soviétique* 31(2/3): 183–91.

Slezkine, Yuri. (1994) "The USSR as a Communal Apartment, or how a Socialist State Promoted Ethnic Particularism," *Slavic Review* 53(2): 414–52.

Sokolovskiy, Sergey. (2012) "Writing the History of Russian Anthropology," in Albert Baiburin, Catriona Kelly and Nikolai Vakhtin (eds.) *Russian Cultural Anthropology after the Collapse of Communism*. London: Routledge, 25–49.

Solonari, Vladimir. (2003) "Creating a 'People': A Case Study in Post-Soviet History-Writing," *Kritika: Explorations in Russian and Eurasian History* 4(2): 411–38.

Suny, Ronald Grigor. (2001) "Constructing Primordialism: Old Histories and New Nations," *The Journal of Modern History* 73(4): 862–96.

Tishkov, Valery Aleksandrovich. (2003) *Rekviem po etnosu – issledovaniia po sotsial'no-kul'turnoi antropologii*. Moskva: Nauka.

Tishkov, Valery Aleksandrovich. (1997) *Ethnicity, Nationalism and Conflict in and after the Soviet Union: The Mind Aflame*. London: Sage.

Tishkov, Valery Aleksandrovich. (1992) "The Crisis in Soviet Ethnography," *Current Anthropology* 33(4): 371–94.
Tokarew, Sergej Aleksandrovič. (1954) "Die nationale Politik der Sowjetunion und die Aufgaben und Erfolge der sowjetischen Ethnographie," *Völkerforschung - Vorträge der Tagung für Völkerkunde an der Humboldt-Universität Berlin vom 25.-27. April 1952*. Berlin: Akademie Verlag, 7–22.
Wanner, Catherine. (1998) *Burden of Dreams: History and Identity in Post-Soviet Ukraine*. University Park PA: The Pennsylvania State University Press.

# ISSUES IN THE HISTORY AND MEMORY OF THE OUN II

GUEST EDITED BY

YULIYA YURCHUK AND ANDREAS UMLAND

# Introduction:
# Essays in the Historical Interpretation of the Organization of Ukrainian Nationalists

Yuliya Yurchuk and Andreas Umland

This is the second installment of a series of thematic *JSPPS* sections dedicated to the memory and history of the Organization of Ukrainian Nationalists (OUN) as well as its military arm, the Ukrainian Insurgent Army (UPA).[1] The present foreword is also the second introduction to this topic. It is thus shorter than, and will not repeat what we have already outlined in, the first special section's introduction which is freely available online.[2]

The papers of the first section focused on some contentious issues in the memory of the OUN-UPA and their comparatively informed interpretation.[3] They also tackled questions of these

---

[1] *JSPPS* herewith invites proposals for further special sections for its subseries "Issues in the History and Memory of the OUN." Such proposals' contents and composition should follow the example of the two paper collections presented in the previous *JSPPS* issue and here.

[2] Andreas Umland and Yuliya Yurchuk, "Introduction: The Organization of Ukrainian Nationalists (OUN) in Post-Soviet Ukrainian Memory Politics, Public Debates, and Foreign Affairs," *Journal of Soviet and Post-Soviet Politics and Society* 3, no. 2 (2017): 115–28, https://www.academia.edu/36059737/The_Organization_of_Ukrainian_Nationalists_OUN_in_Post_Soviet_Ukrainian_Memory_Politics_Public_Debates_and_Foreign_Affairs (accessed 16 April 2018). This second introduction, like the one to the first special section within this series, does not list many of the previous scholarly studies on this section's topic in as far as most of the relevant articles and books are listed in the two special sections' papers' footnotes. We are very grateful to Julie Fedor for her extremely careful and patient final editing of the contributions to these two special sections (including this introduction). Responsibility for any remaining imprecisions and misinterpretations here and below lies, however, solely with the respective texts' authors.

[3] Per Anders Rudling, "Yushchenko's Fascist: The Bandera Cult in Ukraine and Canada;" Yaroslav Hrytsak, "Ukrainian Memory Culture Post-1991: The Case of Stepan Bandera;" Yuliya Yurchuk, "Rivne's Memory of Taras Bul'ba-Borovets': A

organizations' adequate ethical assessment and the contemporary use of their history against the background of the Russian-Ukrainian war since 2014.[4] This section has similar general foci, yet deals with some different subthemes in the OUN's and UPA's history as well as their legacy for present day Ukraine.[5]

The political scientist Ivan Gomza (Kyiv-Mohyla Academy) offers a sociological explanation for the expansion of radical nationalist sentiments and the reinforcement of Ukrainian radical nationalist movements in the Second Polish Republic from 1918 through the 1930s.[6] He argues that, under the specific conditions of this period, a particular political opportunity structure unfolded that became more and more beneficial to the effectiveness and popularity of the radical politics represented by the OUN. These novel conditions allowed the OUN to turn from a fringe phenomenon into the most decisive political force, among Ukrainians in Poland, that even

---

Regional Perspective on the Formation of the Founding Myth of the UPA;" and Lukasz Adamski, "Kyiv's 'Volhynian Negationism': Reflections on the 2016 Polish–Ukrainian Memory Conflict," *Journal of Soviet and Post-Soviet Politics and Society* 3, no. 2 (2017): 129–290.

[4] See also, earlier in this journal, on the same topic, the following review essays on Grzegorz Rossoliński-Liebe, *Stepan Bandera: The Life and Afterlife of a Ukrainian Nationalist. Fascism, Genocide, and Cult* (Stuttgart: *ibidem*-Verlag, 2014), by: Oleksandr Zaitsev, "De-Mythologizing Bandera: Towards a Scholarly History of the Ukrainian Nationalist Movement;" André Härtel, "Bandera's Tempting Shadow: The Problematic History of Ukrainian Radical Nationalism in the Wake of the Maidan;" and Yuri Radchenko, "From Staryi Uhryniv to Munich: The First Scholarly Biography of Stepan Bandera," *Journal of Soviet and Post-Soviet Politics and Society* 1, no. 2 (2015): 411–58.

[5] These English-language collections run in parallel to a related larger 2016–2018 multi-author Russian-language project comprising four special sections on the history and memory of the OUN-UPA in volumes 13–15 (issues 26–29) of the Bavaria-based web-journal *Forum noveishei vostochnoevropeiskoi istorii i kul'tury* (Forum for Contemporary East European History and Culture), with contributions by, among others, Timothy D. Snyder, Yaroslav Hrytsak, John-Paul Himka, Myroslav Shkandrij, Grzegorz Motyka, Oleksandr Zaitsev, Kai Struve, Heorhii Kas'ianov, Per Anders Rudling, and others—some of them also contributors here. See http://www1.ku-eichstaett.de/ZIMOS/forumruss.html (accessed 16 April 2018).

[6] See, also in English language: Ivan Gomza, "Elusive Proteus: A Study in the Ideological Morphology of the Organization of Ukrainian Nationalists," *Communist and Post-Communist Studies* 48, nos. 2–3 (2015): 195–207.

partially suppressed other parties. The author presents five indicators of the specific political opportunity structure that facilitated the increasing legitimacy, reach and persuasiveness of radical (rather than more moderate) Ukrainian nationalism in inter-war Poland. Gomza introduces the concept of "catalytic mobilization," a type of mobilization that occurs despite governmental attempts to restrain it. Thanks to such catalytic mobilization, the author argues, the OUN overtook other Ukrainian nationalist groups active in the inter-war period.

The Russian historian Igor Barinov (IMEMO) tackles the particularly difficult and controversial question of the occurrence, kind, degree, frequency and magnitude of Ukrainian collaboration with the Third Reich, in Eastern Europe's occupied territories, during World War II. As Barinov demonstrates, there is no simple answer to the question about the nature, motives and aims of Ukrainian collaboration. Barinov outlines why researchers dealing with this issue of collaboration have to take into consideration diverse factors. Thus, there are differing drivers of the behavior of populations that have to interact with an occupying power. There was even considerable difference between various interactions between Nazi authorities and Ukrainian nationalists—not to mention those with common people stuck in the occupied territory.

The purpose of collaboration of nationalists and the general population ranged from ideologically motivated behavior to merely situational decisions to cooperate dictated by the desire to survive or to improve one's status under the peculiar circumstances of occupation. Moreover, there was no stable and coherent approach to the future of the occupied territories among the Nazis whose policies were oscillating between the (moderate) "Ostministerium line," potentially allowing the establishment of some Ukrainian autonomy, and the (brutal) "SS-line," aiming to merely utilize the guerrilla experience of Ukrainian radical nationalists for the fight against the Soviets—and then eliminate the collaborators once they were no longer needed. There were profound misunderstandings, numerous miscalculations, and widespread situational thinking within all parties related to the collaboration exercise.

Barinov also deals with the widely accepted view that the local population eagerly welcomed Germans. He draws attention to the fact that, by the time of the German advance into the USSR, many people in Ukraine were disoriented as, in a short period of time from June 1939 to June 1941, the Soviet state propaganda had changed its position towards the Germans three times—from "fascists" to "strategic allies" again to "fascists." When approaching the Nazis' relations to the two factions of OUN, the Melnykites and Banderites, one also has to take into account the diverse facets of the Ukrainian nationalist factions' varying motivations and types of interaction. The author concludes that one cannot easily speak about collaboration per se or only about one type of alliance between the Nazis and OUN, as the situation was complex and had many nuances making a clear-cut and encompassing evaluation of the relations between the Third Reich and Ukrainian collaborators a difficult task.

In his chapter, Myroslav Shkandrij (University of Manitoba) reviews Volodymyr Viatrovych's, in Ukraine, influential, yet, outside Ukraine, highly controversial *Second Polish–Ukrainian War*.[7] Shkandrij's critique illustrates how Viatrovych's work is designed to serve not so much cognitive as propagandistic purposes within the current memory politics in post-Soviet Ukraine.[8] As Shkandrij shows, Viatrovych's book was written using several new and unpublished archival sources, but nevertheless misses the opportunity to present an innovative exploration of Polish–Ukrainian relations during the war-time and inter-war periods. The book succumbs to

---

[7] See also: Myroslav Shkandrij, *Ukrainian Nationalism: Politics, Ideology, and Literature, 1929–1956* (New Haven, CT: Yale University Press, 2015); and Heather Coleman, Yaroslav Hrytsak, Tamara Hundorova, Oleksandr Zaitsev and Myroslav Shkandrij, "A Roundtable on Myroslav Shkandrij's *Ukrainian Nationalism: Politics, Ideology, and Literature, 1929–1956*," *Canadian Slavonic Papers - Revue Canadienne des Slavistes* 59, nos. 1–2 (2017): 131–52.

[8] Shkandrij's critical assessment partly continues an earlier discussion of Viatrovych's controversial book, in the quarterly *Ab Imperio*. See: Sofia Grachova, "Introduction to the Forum;" Per Anders Rudling, "Warfare or War Criminality?;" Igor' Il'iushin, "Plokho zabytoe staroe: o novoi knige Vladimira Viatrovicha;" Gzhegozh [Grzegorz] Motyka, "Neudachnaia kniga;" Andzhei Zemba [Andrzej Zięba], "Mifologizirovannaia voina;" and Vladimir Viatrovich [Volodymyr Viatrovych], "Vtoraia pol'sko-ukrainskaia voina i diskussii vokrug nee," *Ab Imperio* 12, no. 1 (2012): 351–433.

nationalist biases that lead Viatrovych to ignore various nuances a more neutral consideration of which could have contributed to a better understanding of the difficult history of inter-ethnic conflict during the Nazis' occupation of Eastern Europe.

Shkandrij identifies several problematic aspects in the way Viatrovych's book presents the Polish–Ukrainian conflict. These include the assertion of an equivalence between the killing of Poles in Volhynia and the killing of Ukrainians by Poles; a total identification of the Ukrainian national liberation struggle with the activities of the OUN(b); Viatrovych's tendency to ignore or misrepresent elements in the OUN's political program and ideology; the omission of Ukrainian participation in the Holocaust; Viatrovych's refusal to assign responsibility to the higher leadership the OUN(b) and UPA for the decision to begin the destruction of Poles in Volhynia in 1943, and his reluctance to fully recognize the guilt and responsibility of Ukrainians for the conduct of these massacres. Shkandrij comments on each of these themes adding his own interpretation based on the available sources.

As Shkandrij shows, Viatrovych's text represents a contemporary apology for the OUN(b).[9] A pattern emerges in Viatrovych's widely read book: many groups are made responsible for atrocities, but when it comes to the OUN(b), its violence is either minimized or explained as an allegedly inevitable consequence of the ongoing

---

[9] This should not come as a surprise, as Viatrovych's main non-governmental affiliation is the Center for the Study of the Liberation Movement (Ukr. abbrev.: TsDVR), in L'viv. In the words of an OUN(b) representative: "The Organization [of Ukrainian Nationalists] is today a global (world-wide) closed structure, and much of the [work] done remains unannounced [...]. At the same time, a large segment of [its] activity is known thanks to various façade structures [*zavdiaki riznym fasadnym strukturam*] founded by the OUN: from political [...] to academic [ones, like] the 'Center for the Study of the Liberation Movement' (TsDVR) [...];" Sviatoslav Lypovets'kyi, *Orhanizatsiia ukrainskikh natsionalistiv (banderivtsi): fragmenty diial'nosti ta borot'by* (Kyiv: Ukrains'ka Vydavnycha Spil'ka, 2010), 84. As quoted in: Rudling, "Yushchenko's Fascist," 159. It is also worrisome that, Rudling rightly notes (*ibid.*), as manifestly a partisan organization as the TsDVR has been given control over the National Memory Policy Experts Group within Ukraine's major and otherwise reputed NGO umbrella organization "Reanimation Package of Reforms." See: http://rpr.org.ua/en/groups-rpr/17policy-of-national-memory/ (accessed 16 April 2018).

war. Viatrovych fails to analyze the different shades of guilt, responsibility, and co-responsibility among bystanders and perpetrators, and various forms of individual and collective participation in crimes. His outspokenly apologetic approach is symptomatic of the memory politics conducted by various contemporary Ukrainian publicists and organs, among them the Institute of National Memory, whose director Viatrovych has been since 2014.

As the four research papers of the first special section on the Organization of Ukrainian Nationalists, within the previous *JSPPS* issue,[10] the three articles presented below add to the recent wave of new scholarly publications, on the history and memory of the OUN.[11] They make contributions to the increasingly sophisticated scholarly discussion of OUN's ideas and activities before and during World War II, as well as their contemporary interpretation. At the same time, they constitute important expert interventions into the ongoing Ukrainian public debate about the role of the OUN in and for Ukraine's national history.

---

[10] Rudling, "Yushchenko's Fascist;" Hrytsak, "Ukrainian Memory Culture Post-1991;" Yurchuk, "Rivne's Memory of Taras Bul'ba-Borovets';" and Adamski, "Kyiv's 'Volhynian Negationism'."

[11] For brief surveys of the recent literature, see the review articles: Jared McBride, "Who Is Afraid of Ukrainian Nationalism?" *Kritika: Explorations in Russian and Eurasian History* 17, no. 3 (2016): 647–63; and Per Anders Rudling, "Dispersing the Fog: The OUN and Anti-Jewish Violence in 1941," *Yad Vashem Studies* 44, no. 2 (2016): 227–45.

# Catalytic Mobilization of Radical Ukrainian Nationalists in the Second Polish Republic: The Impact of Political Opportunity Structure

Ivan Gomza

***Abstract:*** *This article brings together historical and political science approaches in order to examine the growth of radical nationalist sentiment and the subsequent strengthening of Ukrainian radical nationalist movements in the Second Polish Republic, from 1918 through the 1930s. Offering a sociological explanation for this process, the article applies the concepts of contentious politics and political opportunity structure to the field of study. The author argues that during the interwar period, contentious politics were used by both the moderate and radical wings of the Ukrainian nationalist movement. However, the moderate nationalists adopted a contained contention strategy, whereas the radical nationalists opted for a transgressive contention strategy. Consequently, their mutual disposition was characterized by an opposite flank effect—a competition for resources between the wings, their common goal notwithstanding.*

*This competition unfolded within a particular political opportunity structure (hereafter: POS) of the Second Polish Republic. Using five indicators of POS, the author suggests that the successful mobilization of the radical Ukrainian nationalists was facilitated by the increasing opening of POS towards the radical strategy. A chronological study of POS fluctuations is used to demonstrate the case.*

*The article also expands the scholarly understanding of mechanisms of contentious politics by introducing the concept of "catalytic mobilization"—an extensive resource mobilization process occurring despite governmental attempts to restrain it. As this study shows, catalytic mobilization was a crucial component in the further strengthening of the position of Ukrainian radical nationalists under the Second Polish Republic.*

## Introduction

Interdisciplinarity is increasingly viewed by historians, sociologists, and political scientists as a prerequisite for analysis with any real relevance, and consequently, scholarly approaches within the different subfields of social science are currently undergoing a process of convergence.[1] Because history and political science complement one another, cross-fertilization of these two disciplines in particular can potentially improve our understanding of historical events. Given this, it is productive to apply political science models to the study of how and why radical nationalism gained ground among Ukrainian citizens of the Second Polish Republic. This paper studies the causal mechanisms that led to the failure of the project for Polish–Ukrainian peaceful coexistence within a single state in the inter-war period. The gradual spread of radical nationalist visions among Ukrainians during this period both illustrated and propelled this failure. In this connection, it is important to understand how Polish attempts to regulate and resolve "the Ukrainian question" through engaging moderate Ukrainians into the political process of the Second Polish Republic contributed to the eventual triumph of Ukrainian radicals.[2] In this article, I argue that in order to understand the discrepancy between the governmental policy and societal reactions, it is useful to pay attention to the dynamic of contention and the shifts in the political opportunity structure during this period.

Ukrainian nationalism of the interwar period is conventionally studied as a political ideology. Typically, scholars work with speeches and publications by Ukrainian nationalists, which they use to decipher the ideas and values of political actors. There are many

---

[1] I include the discipline of history here, since I consider it to be a social science.
[2] These attempts have been studied in some detail; see for example Roman Wysocki, *Organizacja Ukraińskich Nacjonalistów w Polsce w latach 1929–1939* (Lublin: Wydawnictwo Uniwersytetu Marii Curie-Skłodowskiej, 2003); *Orhanizatsiia Ukrayins'kykh Natsionalistiv i Ukrayins'ka Povstans'ka Armiia*, ed. S. Kulchyts'kyi (Kyiv: Naukova Dumka, 2005); Ryszard Tomczyk, *Ukraińskie Zjednoczenie Narodowo-Demokratyczne 1925–1939* (Szczecin: Książnica Pomorska, 2006); and Klyment Fedevych, *Galyts'ki ukrayintsi v Pol'shchi, 1920-1939 rr* (Kyiv: Osnovy, 2009).

excellent studies of this kind,[3] which I find insightful. However, I have a methodological objection to the exclusivist focus on ideologies when it comes to the empirical realm of political process. Within the conventional framework, political competition tends to be misrepresented as a clash of ideas, as a torrent of statements and counterarguments. Yet ideas do not exist in the social world separated from their carriers; political actors do not produce political ideas for the sake of ideologies. Rather, they use and abuse ideas in order to mobilize followers, build coalitions, and achieve practical goals. Consequently, if scholars seek to understand not only the philosophical underpinnings of the political process but also the actual course and development of political competition, they should pay more attention to political factors. It is in this vein that I suggest that the proliferation of Ukrainian radical nationalist visions during the interwar period can fruitfully be studied not as a spreading contagion of ideas, but as an outcome of political processes. To this aim I deliberately eschew focusing on ideas; instead, I apply an approach based on the concept of political opportunity structure to the study of the history of Ukrainian nationalism, with the aim of offering some new perspectives on the phenomenon.

The article proceeds as follows: the first part conceptualizes the theory of contentious politics, with special attention to the model of political opportunity structure and the dynamics of contention. The second part studies how and why the political opportunity structure of the Second Polish Republic helped radical nationalists prevail in Galicia and Volhynia during the interwar period. I argue that a particular mechanism of catalytic mobilization is responsible for the fiasco of the cohabitation project and the ensuing ethnic cleansings.

---

[3] See for example Oleksandr Zaitsev, *Ukrains'kyi intehral'nyi natsionalizm (1920-ti–1930-ti roky): Narysy intelektual'noi istorii* (Kyiv: Krytyka, 2013); and Tomasz Stryjek, *Ukraińska idea narodowa okresu międzywojennego* (Toruń: Wydawnictwo Naukowe Uniwersytetu Mikołaja Kopernika, 2013).

## Theory and Methods: Contentious Politics and Political Opportunity Structure

It is reasonable to claim that during the interwar period most of the political actors that fostered ideas of Ukrainian nationalism in the Second Polish Republic had little choice but to resort to contentious politics. As conceptualized by Charles Tilly, contentious politics refers to "interactions in which actors make claims bearing on someone else's interests in which governments appear either as targets, initiators of claims, or third parties."[4] In this study, I understand contentious politics as an *extra-institutional strategy to promote group interests by confrontational collective action and mobilization of political resources*, with the state apparatus being the most important among these resources. The latter is significant due to the fact that contentious actors crave "public goods"[5] (e.g., legislative change or group entitlements), and the state ensures both appropriation of such goods and the continuation of appropriation.

Unlike conventional political participation, contentious politics is practiced outside the institutional framework. Typically, both citizens and elites pursue desired public goods when they participate in political processes through deliberately constructed institutional structures. For example, democratic regimes create a multitude of institutions (elections, plebiscites, an independent judiciary branch) that regulate social and political competition by channeling it into conventional forms. Likewise, authoritarian regimes build political institutions (a single party, the army, consultative councils) to which any political actor contending for a modicum of political power has to resort.[6]

---

[4] Charles Tilly, *Contentious Performances* (Cambridge and New York: Cambridge University Press, 2008), 5.

[5] Mancur Olson, *The Logic of Collective Action: Public Goods and the Theory of Groups* (Cambridge, MA: Harvard University Press, 2002).

[6] For more on political institutions and their role for authoritarian regimes see: Jennifer Gandhi and Adam Przeworski, "Authoritarian Institutions and the Survival of Autocrats," *Comparative Political Studies* 40, no. 11 (2007): 1279–1301; Brian Lai and Dan Slater, "Institutions of the Offensive: Domestic Sources of Dispute Initiation in Authoritarian Regimes, 1950–1992," *American Journal of Political Science* 50, no. 1 (2006): 113–26; Paul Brooker, *Non Democratic Regimes:*

Nevertheless, sometimes none of the institutional channels can be used for promoting a given group's interests in a satisfying manner. For instance, a unitary state does not allow inhabitants of a region to represent their interests appropriately; elections are rigged under electoral authoritarianism, and so they do not accurately represent citizens' preferences. When conventional ways to shape policy are blocked, political actors can promote their interests exclusively through non-institutional channels. Private individuals can turn to informal practices capable to ensure their interests are met, such as lobbyism, personal ties, and corruption. When it comes to the acquisition of public goods, however, there is only one alternative to conventional politics, namely: contentious politics.

Actors express their discontent and promote their interests through numerous tactics or, as Tilly labeled them, "contentious performances." Citizens can organize mass rallies, sign petitions, launch strikes, boycott officials, stop paying taxes, occupy governmental buildings, self-immolate, organize terrorist acts or political assassinations, or start an insurgency—to name just a few of the available tactics.

In a pioneering study, McAdam, Tarrow, and Tilly distinguished two ideal types of contentious politics: contained contention; and transgressive contention.[7] Despite the criticism which this dichotomy has attracted from some scholars,[8] I find it useful, since it helps to elucidate the dynamics of contention in general and strategic choices made by actors in particular, as this study bears witness. However, in order to retain the dichotomy, I suggest some

---

    *Theory, Government, and Politics* (Basingstoke and New York: Palgrave Macmillan, 2009); and Ivan Gomza, "Multysektoralna klasyfikatsiia avtorytarnykh rezhymiv," *Naukovi zapysky NaUKMA* 160 (2014): 10–17.

[7] Doug McAdam, Sidney Tarrow, and Charles Tilly, *Dynamics of Contention* (Cambridge: Cambridge University Press, 2004), 7–8.

[8] Mark Lichbach, "Contending Theories of Contentious Politics and the Structure-Action Problem of Social Order," *Annual Review of Political Science* 1, no. 1 (1998): 401–24; Kevin O'Brien, "Neither Transgressive nor Contained: Boundary-Spanning Contention in China," *Mobilization* 8, no. 1 (2003): 51–64; and Paul Dosh, *Demanding the Land: Urban Popular Movements in Peru and Ecuador, 1990–2005* (University Park: Pennsylvania State University Press, 2010): 221–23.

further conceptualizations. The definition of transgressive contention by McAdam, Tarrow, and Tilly is rather vague. They deem contention transgressive if "at least some parties to the conflict are newly self-identified political actors, and/or at least some parties employ innovative collective action."[9] This definition is hardly operational, since the novelty of both political actors and collective action will always remain a matter of scholarly discussion. Instead, I suggest drawing a distinction between contained and transgressive contention based on the legal framework of the regime upon which the contentious actors strive to make an impact. Contention is contained when citizens resort to non-institutional, but normatively and legally acceptable confrontational tactics. Alternatively, contention is transgressive when its actors utilize both non-institutional and illegal tactics. My definition suggests that under democratic regimes mass rallies, civic processions, and petitions constitute contained contention (although this might not be true under authoritarianism), whereas under most political regimes terrorism, assassinations, insurrections, and other forms of political violence are transgressive. Nevertheless, the watershed between the two types of contention is not violence per se, but legally and culturally defined norms. Furthermore, the contentious actor must be aware of these norms and their transgression in order for an action to be categorized as transgressive contention. A case in point is Rosa Parks' famed refusal: she intentionally violated the segregation laws, and can thus be said to have resorted to a non-violent transgressive contention. In other words, the type of contentious politics is intertwined with the nature of the given political regime and its legal peculiarities. Nevertheless, in historical perspective, most political regimes lean towards toleration of non-violent contention and even codify it as legally acceptable, while severely penalizing and prohibiting any violent contention. As a result, contained contention tends to be non-violent, whereas violent contention is always transgressive.

    This generalization is heuristically important for the study of Ukrainian nationalism in the Second Polish Republic, for it

---

[9] McAdam, Tarrow, and Tilly, *Dynamics of Contention*, 8.

illustrates, as described below, the strategic challenge faced by nationalists, which stemmed from the practical impossibility of combining the two modes of contention for a long period. Such inability provoked rivalry between moderate and radical Ukrainian nationalists, their ideological affinities notwithstanding.

To further understand the nature of political contention, one should bear in mind that its extra-institutional nature does not mean that it is separate from routinized conventional politics. On the contrary, both forms are constantly interacting, supplementing, amplifying, and contrasting with each other.[10] Even transgressive contention is tightly intertwined with conventional politics.[11] Terrorists, under certain conditions, could be involved in conventional political process and even constitute legal political parties. This trajectory was followed, for instance, by the Lebanese *Hezbollah*.[12] Likewise, insurgent and guerrilla organizations might opt for political solutions and evolve into political parties (e.g. the transformation of the Nicaraguan Sandanistas or Mozambican FRELIMO).[13] Conversely, political parties turn to clandestine activities or political violence when they fail to achieve their goals through conventional politics. For instance, the Turkish *Nationalist Movement Party*

---

[10] Cf.: Doug McAdam and Sidney Tarrow, "Ballots and Barricades: On the Reciprocal Relationship between Election and Social Movements," *Perspectives on Politics* 36 (2010): 529–42; and Edwin Amenta, Neal Caren, Elizabeth Chiarello, and Yang Su, "The Political Consequences of Social Movements," *Annual Review of Sociology* 35, no. 1 (2010): 287-307.

[11] For more on theoretical explanations of transgressive contention and conventional politics see: Ehud Sprinzak, "The Process of Delegitimation: Towards a Linkage Theory of Political Terrorism," *Terrorism and Political Violence* 3, no. 1 (1991): 50–68; Leonard Weinberg, Ami Pedahzur, and Arie Perliger, *Political Parties and Terrorist Groups* (London: Routledge, 2009); Anisseh van Engeland and Rachael Rudolph, *From Terrorism to Politics* (Aldershot, England and Burlington: Ashgate, 2008); James Piazza, "Terrorism and Party Systems in the States of India," *Security Studies* 19 (2010): 99–123; and Orlandrew Danzell, "Political Parties: When Do They Turn to Terror?" *Journal of Conflict Resolution* 55, no. 1 (2010): 85–105.

[12] Eitan Azani, "The Hybrid Terrorist Organization: Hezbollah as a Case Study," *Studies in Conflict & Terrorism* 36, no. 11 (2013): 899–916.

[13] Kalowatie Deonandan, David Close, and Gary Prevost (eds.), *From Revolutionary Movements to Political Parties* (Basingstoke: Palgrave Macmillan, 2007).

launched a wave of terror attacks in the country during the 1970s,[14] and the Japanese *Aum Shinrikyō* turned to terror after its failure in the parliamentary election.[15]

Political actors that practice contained contention are even more likely to participate in conventional politics. The Egyptian *Muslim Brotherhood* is a revealing illustration of strategies used by a social movement to shape political agendas, societal expectations, and the nature of political competition within a given policy.[16] Furthermore, social movements tend to build temporary alliances with political parties, thus helping to mobilize the electorate or even growing into minor coalitional partners.[17] Such assistance is widely sought by conventional political actors, aiming to gain broader political support or extra-institutional leverage over opponents.

The interplay of conventional and contentious politics was decisive for Ukrainian nationalists under the Second Polish Republic. Such organizations as the *Ukrainian Military Organization* (hereafter: UVO, from the Ukrainian initials) during the 1920s and the *Organization of Ukrainian Nationalists* (OUN) during the 1930s were the principal actors employing transgressive contention with the aim of delegitimizing and weakening the Polish state and creating propitious conditions for an independent Ukrainian state. To this purpose, both the UVO and the OUN mobilized material and cultural resources,[18] built informal networks that helped to manage

---

[14] Walter Laqueur, *The New Terrorism: Fanaticism and the Arms of Mass Destruction* (New York: Oxford University Press, 1999), 146.
[15] Ian Reader, *A Poisonous Cocktail? Aum Shinrikyō's Path to Violence* (Copenhagen: NIAS Books, 1996), 67–69.
[16] For more on this see: Noha Antar, "The Muslim Brotherhood's Success in the Legislative Elections in Egypt 2005: Reasons and Implications," *Euro-MeSCo Paper* 51 (2006), http://www.euromesco.net/images/51_eng.pdf; and Carrie Rosefsky Wickham, *The Muslim Brotherhood: Evolution of an Islamist Movement* (Princeton: Princeton University Press, 2015).
[17] McAdam and Tarrow, "Ballots and Barricades": 533.
[18] For more on resource mobilization see: John McCarthy and Mayer Zald, "Resource Mobilization and Social Movements: A Partial Theory," *American Journal of Sociology* 82, no. 6 (1977): 1212–41; Craig Jenkins, "Resource Mobilization Theory and the Study of Social Movements," *Annual Review of Sociology* 9 (1983): 527–53; M. Zald and J. McCarthy, "The Resource Mobilization Research Program: Progress, Challenge, and Transformation" in *New Directions in*

those resources,[19] and constructed alternative frameworks which propagated the negative perception of the Polish domination in Galicia and Volhynia.[20]

The political goals of both the UVO and the OUN were similar to those of other Ukrainian political organizations, the *Ukrainian National Democratic Alliance* (UNDO) being the most prominent among them. The latter is remarkable, for it represented the entangled relations between conventional and contentious politics. On the one hand, UNDO members took part in parliamentary elections in 1928, 1930, 1935, and 1938, and some of them were elected to sit in both the lower house (Sejm) and the Senate. On the other hand, it would be misleading to describe UNDO as having evolved into a full-fledged political party. This claim might seem like an overstatement, so I should substantiate it in some detail. In political science, a political party has been variously defined as "an organized attempt

---

*Contemporary Sociological Theory*, eds. Joseph Berger and Morris Zelditch (Lanham: Rowman & Littlefield Publishers, 2002), 147–71; and B. Edwards and J. McCarthy, "Resources and Social Movement Mobilization" in *The Blackwell Companion to Social Movements*, eds. David Snow, Sarah Soule, and Hanspeter Kriese (Malden: Blackwell Publishing, 2004), 116–52.

[19] The literature on the role of social networks for contentious politics is vast. See, for example: P. Blau, "Structural Sociology and Network Analysis. An Overview" in *Social Structure and Network Analysis*, eds. Peter Marsden and Nan Lin (Beverly Hills: Sage Publications, 1985); Kevin Cook and Joseph Whitmeyer, "Two Approaches to Social Structure: Exchange Theory and Network Analysis," *Annual Review of Sociology* 18 (1992): 109–27; Peter Bearman and Kevin Everett, "The Structure of Social Protest 1961–83," *Social Networks* 15 (1993): 171–200; and Mario Diani and Doug McAdam (eds.), *Social Movements and Networks Relational Approaches to Collective Action* (New York: Oxford University Press, 2003).

[20] On frames and contentious politics see: David Snow, Burke Rochford, Steven Worden, and Robert Benford, "Frame Alignment Processes, Micromobilization, and Movement Participation" *American Sociological Review* 51 (1986): 464–81; D. Snow and R. Benford, "Master Frames and Cycles of Protest" in *Frontiers of Social Movement Theory*, eds. Aldon Morris and Carol Mueller (New Haven, CT: Yale University Press, 1992); Daniel Cress and David Snow, "The Outcomes of Homeless Mobilization: The Influence of Organization, Disruption, Political Mediation, and Framing," *American Journal of Sociology* 105 (2000): 1063–1104; and Rory McVeigh, David Myers, and David Sikkink, "Corn, Klansmen, and Coolidge: Structure and Framing in Social Movements," *Social Forces* 83, no. 2 (2004): 653–90.

to get power";[21] "a group whose members propose to act in concert in the competitive struggle for political power";[22] "a formal organization whose self-conscious, primary purpose is to place and maintain in public office persons who will control [...] the machinery of government";[23] and a group "seeking to elect governmental officeholders under a given label."[24] UNDO met the common criteria of the cited definitions only partially, since it had neither an official label nor formal membership nor a membership roster; moreover, the membership fee was paid only by those who were elected to the parliament,[25] and members themselves viewed electoral campaigns as one of several possible strategies to regulate the "Ukrainian question." Other strategies included the organization of petitions; the development of national self-consciousness (for this purpose UNDO financially supported publication of two major Ukrainian-speaking newspapers, *Liberty (Svoboda)* and *The Act (Dilo)*, as well as numerous books); the funding of various social organizations, *Enlightenment (Prosvita)*, *The Native School (Ridna Shkola)*, and *The Falcon (Sokil)*); and attempts to ensure the economic prosperity of Ukrainians (for this purpose UNDO supported the Ukrainian Cooperative Movement and different economic initiatives like *Maslosoiuz* and *Dnister*). To some extent, UNDO was not a political party, but rather an umbrella organization which facilitated cooperation between different participants of Ukrainian social, economic, and political life under the Second Polish Republic. Therefore, UNDO was first and foremost an actor of contentious politics.

The numerous points of contact between UNDO representatives and the UVO and, later, OUN militants, support my interpretation. Moreover, there was little ideological difference between

---

[21] Elmer Schnattschneider, *Party Government* (New York: Holt, Rinehart and Winston, 1942), 35.
[22] Joseph Schumpeter, *Capitalism, Socialism, and Democracy* (New York: Harper and Row, 1943), 196.
[23] Joseph LaPalombara, *Politics Within Nations* (Englewood Cliffs: Prentice Hall, 1974), 509.
[24] Leon Epstein. *Political Parties in Western Democracies* (London: Pall Mall, 1967), 9.
[25] Osyp Nazaruk, *Hohy i Mahohy: polytychna broshura pryznachena dlia hartuvannia buduchykh ukrains'kykh providnykiv* (L'viv: [n.e.], 1936), 56.

UNDO and UVO/OUN, since all three organizations strived for an independent Ukrainian state. This is the main reason why UVO/OUN members often met, held discussions, and sought for common ground with UNDO people;[26] some individuals, like Dmytro Paliiv, even simultaneously held membership in both UVO and UNDO. As a matter of fact, during the 1920s UNDO and UVO were mutually complementary: the former acted as moderate political opposition, the latter was a clandestine militant organization, and their cooperation helped to push for their common goal. Such partnership is commonly observed in contentious politics: for instance, the *African National Congress* or many feminist organizations had their militarized wings. There is a strategical reason for such partnership: a regime facing simultaneously contained and transgressive contention tends to make some concession to moderate actors, whose claims are usually acceptable for or even formulated in concert with the radicals. In the scholarly literature, this cooperation is described as the "radical flank effect."[27] Due to the radical flank effect, UVO members held sway over UNDO policy proposals,[28] to the point where by the 1930s the UVO leader, Yevhen Konovalets', decided to amplify the mutual complementarity of the political and military wings through inauguration of the OUN.[29]

---

[26] There is evidence of active communication between UNDO representatives (e.g. Levyts'kyi, Rudnyts'kyi, Kedryn) and UVO/OUN members (Konovalets', Sushko, Holovins'kyi). For more information consult: Ryszard Torzecki, *Kwestia ukraińska w Polsce w latach 1923-1929* (Kraków: Wydawnictwo Literackie, 1989), 338–40; and Zaitsev, *Ukrains'kyi intehral'nyi natsionalizm*, 299–303.

[27] See: Jo Freeman, *The Politics of Women's Liberation: A Case Study of an Emerging Social Movement and its Relation to the Policy Process* (New York: McKay, 1975); Herbert Haines, "Black Radicalization and the Funding of Civil Rights: 1957–1970," *Social Problems* 32, no. 1 (1984): 31–43; Devashree Gupta, "Radical Flank Effects: The Effect of Radical-Moderate Splits in Regional Nationalist Movements," *Paper prepared for the Conference of Europeanists*, Chicago: 14–16 March 2002; and Kurt Schock, *Unarmed Insurrections: People Power Movements in Nondemocracies* (Minneapolis: Minnesota University Press, 2005).

[28] Osyp Navrots'kyi, "UVO, politychna partiia, dyktatura ZOUNR ta uriad UNR," in *Ievhen Konovalets' i ioho doba*, ed. Iurii Boyko (Miunkhen: Vydannia Fundatsii im. Ievhena Konovaltsia, 1974), 299.

[29] Cf. memoirs and testimonies by Ukrainian nationalists: Volodymyr Ianiv, "Zustrich z polkovnykom Konoval'tsem na tli nastroiiv doby," in *Ievhen Konovalets' i ioho doba*, ed. Iurii Boyko (Munich: Vydannia Fundatsii im. Ievhena

There was, however, a tactical rift between the radicals and the moderates: UNDO deemed violent means to be unacceptable. The social milieus of UNDO's sympathizers generally preferred a blend of political moderation and nationalism. Many adherents joined UNDO after a prolonged membership in the left-liberal *Ukrainian Popular Working Party* or the centrist *Ukrainian Party of the National Work,* thus being impregnated with moderate values. The center-liberal stance combined with a deliberate strategic choice had eventually pushed UNDO to embrace a so-called "loyalist policy" (*uhodovstvo*) towards the Polish establishment, which provoked an overt rupture and intense competition with OUN in the mid–1930s. The quest for political understanding with the Polish authorities did not mean that the UNDO had abandoned its ultimate goal, the achievement of Ukrainian statehood; rather, the organization decided to wait for more favorable conditions, meanwhile focusing on legal tactics in its effort to promote the interests of Ukrainians.[30] However, the strategic cooperation with the Polish establishment enraged UNDO's radical partner, the OUN, and the two organizations clashed as a result.

The foundation for the confrontation was laid by a discrepancy in tactics: while UNDO opted for contained contention, OUN considered this useless and insisted on transgressive contention. This was a turning point, a moment when the radical flank effect lost its spell, for instead of a thorough and mutually beneficial game against the Polish authorities, the moderate and the radicals started to compete for material and cultural resources required to bring into reality the optimal (from the vantage point of each party) strategy. I label such a competition *the opposite flank effect.*

The opposite flank effect stems from practical difficulties faced by any contentious actor attempting to resort simultaneously to both transgressive and contained contention. When the former is practiced, the actor leaves the domain of legality; therefore, the

---

Konoval'tsia, 1974): 454–55; Stepan Lenkavs'kyi, *Ukraiins'kyi natsionalizm: tvory,* t. 1 (Ivano-Frankivsk: Lileia, 2002): 128–29.

[30] Paweł Sekuła, "Ukraińskie organizacje i partie polityczne w Drugiej Rzeczypospolitej (do 1926 roku)," *Nowa Ukraina: zeszyty historyczno-politologiczne* 2 (2006): 30.

available reservoir of activists shrinks considerably, because far more people would join a legally acceptable mass rally than would participate in illegal and punishable bombings of governmental buildings, for example. On the other hand, should contained contention be practiced when there is an option (or experience) of transgressive contention, this can provoke a crisis of movement identity and subsequent loss of activists, because radicalized participants deem legal tactics ineffective and meaningless. Thus, there are two gravity points, one attracting moderates and the other, radicals. When each party considers the other not as a partner, but as a rival for a resource pool (that is: when both parties attempt to mobilize the same resources), the opposite flank effect kicks in.

This article examines the social mechanisms responsible for the eventual victory of the strategy employed by radical Ukrainian nationalists during their competition with the moderate Ukrainian nationalists. Attention to social mechanisms, "frequently occurring and easily recognizable causal pattern[s],"[31] has gained priority in the recent methodological approaches to the study of contentious politics.[32] "Victory," as it is understood in this study, refers not to the ultimate goal (formation of an independent Ukraine), but rather to a proximate success: effective resource mobilization and the ensuing discrediting of the rival strategy as a viable alternative in the eyes of the Ukrainian population.

---

[31] Jon Elster, *Explaining Social Behavior* (New York: Cambridge University Press, 2007), 36.
[32] On social mechanisms see: P. Hedström and R. Swedberg, "Social Mechanisms: An Introductory Essay" in *Social Mechanisms: An Analytical Approach to Social Theory*, eds. Peter Hedström and Richard Swedberg (New York: Cambridge University Press, 2005), 24–25. On the particular methodological importance of mechanisms within the field of contentious politics: Charles Tilly, "Mechanisms in Political Processes," *Annual Review of Political Science* 4 (2001): 21–41; Charles Tilly and Sidney Tarrow, *Contentious Politics* (Oxford: Oxford University Press, 2015), 211–19; Doug McAdam, Sidney Tarrow, and Charles Tilly, "Comparative Perspectives on Contentious Politics" in *Comparative Politics: Rationality, Culture, and Structure*, eds. Mark Lichbach and Alan Zuckerman (Cambridge: Cambridge University Press, 2009), 260–62; Eitan Alimi, Lorenzo Bosi, and Chares Demetriou, "Relational Dynamics and Processes of Radicalization," *Mobilization* 17, no. 1 (2012): 9; and Kevin Grisham, *Transforming Violent Political Movements* (London and New York: Routledge, 2014), 31–36.

I argue that political opportunity structure (hereafter: POS) was one of the predominant reasons for the success of radical Ukrainian nationalists. POS is a theoretical model that links the ebbs and flows of resource mobilization and, therefore, the dynamics of contention, to exogeneous factors. Although the idea that causes, forms, and outcomes of contention ultimately depend on economic, demographic, and political systems might seem to be rather self-evident, the POS model formalizes the general intuition about causal relations and generates a set of falsifiable hypotheses. Some scholarly critique of the model notwithstanding,[33] I believe the elaborated form of the model to be meaningful enough to serve as an explanatory tool for the victory of radical Ukrainian nationalists under the Second Polish Republic.

In general terms, the POS model assumes contentious politics to be affected by components of a given political environment (e.g. regime, form of state, or political rights available to contentious actors). In early conceptualizations on the model, McAdam argues that POS influences contention the most when there are shifts in political opportunities;[34] the opening of POS produces both contention and its dynamics. Further formalizing the model, Tarrow suggests that there are four key components of POS: interactions between authorities and contentious actors; the contentious actor's access to participation in political process; availability of political alignments; and division of political elites.[35] In short, Tarrow argues that a given POS is open when (1) governmental policies and political opposition's alternatives barely satisfy some social sectors; when (2) a political system is open enough to participation of non-institutionalized actors (e.g. new social movements); when (3) claims of a newly-arrived actor are supported to some extent by institutional allies (e.g. local administration, the Church, the army); and when

---

[33] For the most recent critique see: Jeff Goodwin and James M. Jasper (eds.), *Contention in Context: Political Opportunities and the Emergence of Protest* (Palo Alto, CA: Stanford University Press, 2012).
[34] Doug McAdam, *Political Process and the Development of Black Insurgency* (Chicago, IL: University of Chicago Press, 1982), 41.
[35] Sidney Tarrow, *Power in Movement: Social Movements and Contentious Politics* (Cambridge: Cambridge University Press, 2011), 164–65.

(4) the elite winning coalition is divided with regards to possible reactions to the contentious actor's claims. When POS is open, it is easier for the contentious actor to mobilize resources, exert pressure upon the authorities, and achieve desired public goods. A classical illustration of the validity of McAdam's and Tarrow's conceptualizations is the US Civil Rights Movement. Its activists were not content with either Democrat or Republican policy proposals; the President and the Attorney General were sympathetic to their claims; the US political system was conducive to civic activities; and the ruling elite were both indecisive and divided with regard how to react to the contentious politics. Consequently, the Civil Rights Movement managed to mobilize enough resources and achieve their desired outcomes.

Tilly elaborated the model further and argued that there are six components of POS: openness of regime; repression; coherence of elite; stability of political alignments; availability of allies; and pace of change.[36] I will use these components as indicators to analyze the shifts in POS during the Second Polish Republic. Tilly's $3^{rd}$, $4^{th}$, and $5^{th}$ indicators correspond to those of Tarrow discussed earlier, while the $6^{th}$ indicator is a contextually dependent variable. However, the role of political regime and that of political repression as POS components require additional discussion. Indeed, political regime (a set of formal and informal rules identifying the political power holders and the nature of their interaction with the population[37]) and political repressions (actions that inhibit resource mobilization by raising the costs of collective action[38]) are intertwined, since different types of political regimes resort to different types of repression and do so with varying intensity.

---

[36] Charles Tilly, *Contentious Performances* (Cambridge and New York: Cambridge University Press, 2008), 91–93.
[37] Svend-Erik Skaaning, "Political Regimes and Their Changes: A Conceptual Framework," *Center on Democracy, Development, and the Rule of Law* Working Paper 55 (2006): 15.
[38] Cf: Charles Tilly, *From Mobilization to Revolution* (Reading: Addison-Wesley Publishing Corporation, 1978), 100; and Brett Stockdill, *Activism against AIDS: At the Intersection of Sexuality, Race, Gender, and Class* (Boulder, CO: Lynne Rienner Publishers, 2003).

Political sociology has established causality between the level of repression under a political regime and the scope of political contention. Contrary to conventional wisdom, contentious politics seldom occurs under highly repressive regimes, capable of suppressing most forms of popular discontent. Likewise, contentious politics is infrequent under non-repressive regimes, because they typically build satisfactory institutional frameworks for funneling popular claims into conventional politics. Thus, there is a so-called curvilinear relationship between political repressions and contentious politics:[39] political contention is more pronounced and intense under semi-repressive regimes (e.g. non-consolidated democracy, anocracy, or electoral authoritarianism), because such regimes tend to accommodate some societal claims, but repress others. Since the responses of semi-repressive regimes lack consistency, various collective actors expect their claims to be granted and they resort to political contention ever more frequently. A regime's accountability to the society is an additional explanation for the curvilinear paradox: non-accountable repressive regimes ignore popular wishes altogether and penalize any contentious claims; accountable non-repressive regimes depend on civic participation, so they encourage citizens to make their preferences obvious, so it is less costly to utilize conventional politics; but semi-accountable regimes, being simultaneously attentive to some societal needs and oblivious to others, provide additional incentives for citizens to voice their dissent and push desirable changes through contentious politics.

Another theoretical assumption stipulates that POS is not the objective reality for societal actors. Rather, as Tarrow aptly explains, POS is also comprised of "dimensions of the political environment

---

[39] This relation is graphically represented by an inverted U-curve which the reader can see on Scheme 1 below. On theoretical explanations of the curvilinear correlation see: Peter Eisinger, "The Conditions of Protest in American Cities," *American Political Science Review* 67, no. 1 (1973): 14; Edward Muller and Mitchell Seligson, "Inequality and Insurgency," *American Political Science Review* 81, no. 2 (1987): 429; Charles Brockett, *Political Movements and Violence in Central America* (Cambridge: Cambridge University Press, 2005), 266–91; and Stephen Shellman, Brian Levey, and Joseph Young, "Shifting Sands: Explaining and Predicting Phase Shifts by Dissident Organizations," *Journal of Peace Research* 50, no. 3 (2013): 319–36.

or changes in that environment that provide incentives for collective action by affecting expectations for success or failure."[40] I concur with this interpretation, because the nature of political regime, the threat of repressions, possible alliances, and even elite cohesion are not empirical facts, but rather perceptions and matters for interpretation. In this study, I understand POS as collective perceptions of what might be effectively done under given political circumstances to promote societal claims. In other words, POS is a combination of the five discussed indicators that serve as social lenses through which contentious actors comprehend the sources of their deprivation, available resources, the level of threats, and whether conditions are auspicious to a contentious campaign. Next, contentious actors utilize this perception to define the most effective strategy, compose an appropriate repertoire of contention, and test out contentious performances in the real world. Therefore, *POS is open when contentious actors perceive their chances of success as relatively high, and, concurrently, the more confident contentious actors are, the more open for their activities POS is.*

The way a given political regime reacts to a given episode of contention is a vital component of perceptions regarding POS. If the regime uses tear gas to suppress a non-violent demonstration, this signalizes closed POS; conversely, when a government starts peace-talks with a terrorist organization, the contentious actor interprets such an initiative as a sign that POS is open. In other words, the regime's reaction to chosen contentious performances is an indicator which helps contentious actors grasp whether their chances of success are growing or shrinking, and whether they should stick to a chosen strategy. When the expectation of prevailing rises, contentious actors intensify their strategy.

Finally, with each successive episode of contention, political elites are more vulnerable to some contentious performances. Under some circumstances, a government wishing to prove that it is in control of the situation might vigorously suppress a non-violent mass rally; but the very same government might make substantial

---

[40] Sidney Tarrow, *Power in Movement: Social Movements and Contentious Politics* (Cambridge: Cambridge University Press, 2011), 163.

concessions to transgressive contention that threatens to fragment the winning coalition and bring about the demise of the regime. Under other circumstances, a government might severely penalize all forms of political violence but seek a compromise with moderate contentious actors. The variety of regime responses exerts selective pressure on both radical and moderates. Selective pressure is the cause of the opposite flank effect. If the regime reveals its vulnerability exclusively to contained or transgressive contention, this might provoke a resource surplus for a successful contentious actor. But because the revelation of regime vulnerabilities comes with a considerable time lag, for a certain period of time radicals and moderates are locked in a fray of probes and interpretations as to whose strategy is really the more effective.

To summarize, there are four theoretical assumptions underpinning this study:

1. Contentious politics is an extra-institutional form of confrontational collective action and mobilization of political resources utilized by societal groups to promote their interests;
2. There are two ideal types of contentious politics, namely contained and transgressive contention—the former encompasses legally and normatively accepted contentious performances, whereas the latter involves resorting to illegal ones;
3. The dynamic of contention is shaped by the political opportunity structure, the latter being a system of links between strategic attempts by contentious actors to promote their interests, their perceptions of the chances of success, and reactions by the political regime to these attempts. There are five empirically measurable indicators of a political opportunity structure: openness of regime, repression, coherence of elite, stability of political alignments, and availability of allies;
4. A political opportunity structure creates selective pressure on actors of both contained and transgressive contention, which, in turn, produces the opposite flank effect—strategic

competition between moderates and radicals who have the same political goal, but compete for available material and cultural resources.

The last thesis is a concise description of the situation faced by the Ukrainian nationalists under the Second Polish Republic. The following section studies how the political opportunity structure in this particular case helped the radicals to prevail.

## Political Opportunity Structure for Ukrainian Nationalists under the Second Polish Republic

In order to study the dynamic interactions between Ukrainian nationalists and the authorities of the Second Polish Republic, I distinguish four periods: (1) original impenetrability (1918–19); (2) the age of parliament (1919–26); (3) Sanation (1926–30); and (4) pacification and normalization (1930–38). These periods are distinguished by particular POS configurations. During each period, selective pressure on radicals and moderates took different forms, which shaped two forms of contention and, in the final account, activated the mechanism of catalytic mobilization for radicals. My arguments are illustrated by Scheme 1 (below). On the scheme, the vertical axis represents *intensity of contentious politics*; the horizontal axis represents *the regime's vulnerability to political contention*; finally, the inverted U-curve traces *how open or closed the POS is* (a higher point corresponds to a more open POS).

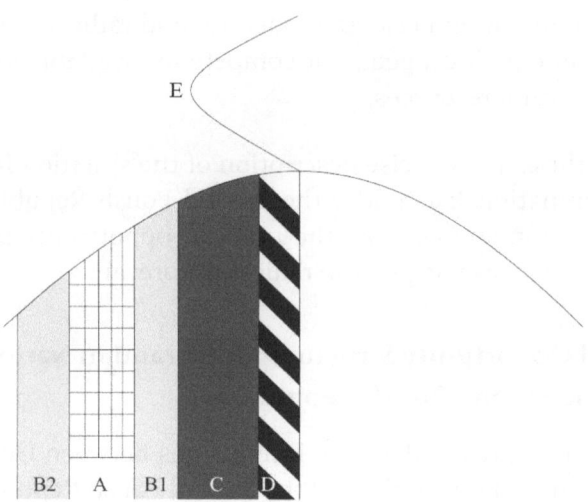

*Scheme 1. Shifts in Political Opportunity Structure for Ukrainian Nationalists under the Second Polish Republic*

## 1. Original Impenetrability (1918–19)

After decades of partition, an independent Poland came into being in the aftermath of World War I. The newly recreated state was involved in territorial conflicts virtually everywhere on its geographical periphery. Poland competed with Germany for Upper Silesia in the west; it clashed with Lithuania over the Vilnius and the Suwalki regions in the north; there was a conflict with Czechoslovakia over Cieszyn Silesia and Orava territory in the south; it waged a full-fledged war against the West Ukrainian People's Republic over Galicia in the east. To compound these challenges even further, ethnic minorities that inhabited the territories incorporated into the Polish state accepted the reestablishment of Polish statehood with substantial reservations. For instance, Masurians in Eastern Prussia preferred citizenship of industrially developed Germany to that of Poland with an uncertain future. As a result, up to 97.5% of them voted against inclusion of their region to Poland during the Warmia,

Masuria, and Powiśle plebiscite.[41] Ślůnzoki, the dominant ethnicity in Upper Silesia, also opted for Germany during the Upper Silesia plebiscite in March 1921.[42] Because neither Poland nor Germany was fully satisfied with the attempts to resolve the "Silesian question," the territorial conflict escalated to clashes between pro-Polish and pro-German militias. The conflict was settled only in October 1921 by the intervention of the League of Nations. Finally, the Jewish minority, which comprised up to 10% of the entire population, was equally unenthusiastic about the new Polish statehood because Polish authorities opposed the Jewish hopes for creating a Jewish autonomy.[43]

Given the circumstances, the key diplomatic achievement of the new state—the fact that the international community recognized the preeminence of Polish rights over those of most of the contested territories—engendered significant political challenges. The most immediate of these was the question of how to ensure the political loyalty of ethnic minorities. This challenge proved to be ever more vital during the Polish–Soviet War when a significant portion of ethnic minorities expected the Polish state to be destroyed and adopted anti-Polish attitudes.

Responding to this challenge, Polish authorities tried to minimize the political and social role of ethnic minorities during the early period of the Second Polish Republic. In practical terms, this led to repression against ethnic minorities. Although these varied in form (there were confiscations of German property in the western regions, anti-Jewish pogroms in Pinsk, a prohibition on studying at universities for those Ukrainians who had not served in the Polish army), the repressions of 1918–19 shared the aims of hindering political mobilization of minorities, minimizing their capability to stage

---

[41] H.-W. Rautenberg, "Probleme der Volksabstimmung vom 11. Juli 1920 im südlichen Ermland und in Masuren" in *Deutschland und das Recht auf nationale Selbstbestimmung nach dem Ersten Weltkrieg. Probleme der Volksabstimmungen im Osten, 1918–1922*, eds. Helmut Neubach, Hans-Werner Rautenberg, and Richard Breyer (Bonn: Kulturstiftung der deutschen Vertriebenen, 1985), 75–91.

[42] Tomasz Kamusella, "Upper Silesia, 1870-1920: Between Region, Religion, Nation and Ethnicity," *East European Quarterly* XXXVIII, no. 4 (2005): 445.

[43] Ezra Mendelsohn, *The Jews of East Central Europe Between the World Wars* (Bloomington, IN: Indiana University Press, 2001), 34–35.

and to coordinate anti-Polish contentious politics, and coercing minorities into submission. Moreover, during the first years of the independence Polish elites were notoriously united by patriotic élan, and no significant social institution supported the contention of Germans, Ukrainians, Masurians, or Jews who became citizens of the Second Polish Republic against their will. Therefore, during the first years of the Polish statehood the POS indicators signaled closure to any contentious claims voiced by ethnic minorities, including Ukrainian nationalists. During the period of original impenetrability, selective pressure concurrently decreased the effectiveness of both contained and transgressive contention. Hence, *in 1918–19 the POS was closed for both moderate and radical Ukrainian nationalists.* (The A-zone and the corresponding section of the inverted U-curve illustrate this period on Scheme 1.)

## 2. Age of Parliament (1919–26)

In January 1919, Ignacy Paderewski assumed office as Prime Minister of the Second Polish Republic. In this post Paderewski substituted a Socialist Jędrzej Moraczewski whom many Polish patriots deemed unreliable by virtue of his ideological partisanship. As a nationalist Paderewski was much more acceptable. Before long, the right-wing ruling elites initiated a new Constitution (1921) that established the Polish state as a parliamentary republic with Prime Minister as the chief executive office. Between 1919 and 1926 this post was usually held by politicians leaning towards the right side of the political spectrum, like Wincenty Witos, Leopold Skulski, and Władysław Grabski. The Polish Right controlled the executive branch due to its domination in the parliament, which, according to the new Constitution, appointed the cabinet. Between 1919 and 1922 the *Popular National Union* (*Związek Ludowo-Narodowy*) was the biggest fraction in parliament. After 1922, ZLN yielded its supremacy to the rightist coalition Chjeno-Piast that included the *Christian Union of National Unity* (*Chrześcijański Związek Jedności Narodowej*) and the *Polish People's Party "Piast"* (*Polskie Stronnictwo Ludowe "Piast"*). To put it succinctly, the Polish political Right dominated during the whole period of parliamentary rule.

Still, the rightists winning coalitions tried different governmental policies to deal with minority questions. Sometimes, they attempted to accommodate minorities; on other occasions, their aim was to force them into compliance. These alterations produced shifts in the POS, which fluctuated between being opened and being closed. These shifts significantly affected all strands of Ukrainian nationalism.

After the military crash of the West Ukrainian People's Republic in June–July 1919, the Polish rule in Eastern Galicia became a *fait accompli*, which significantly decreased the effectiveness of both contained and transgressive contention. Although supporters of the Ukrainian state continued the struggle by practicing guerrilla warfare in the rural areas, the authorities significantly empowered courts-martial in the year 1920. This measure enabled effective, although brutal, pacification of the Ukrainian countryside. Thus, transgressive contention had been effectively repressed. Moderate Ukrainians aimed to convince the international community that the Polish rule in Galicia was illegitimate. To prove it, they utilized classical tactics of contained contention, namely mass rallies, strikes, and boycotts. For instance, they organized a huge demonstration of Ukrainian railway workers with a call to release all political prisoners in February–March 1921, and boycotted the universal census in October 1921. However, after the Peace of Riga (March 1921) the new eastern borders of the Polish state were not only recognized by international law but also enjoyed geopolitical significance in the eyes of the West. With the growing perception of Poland as a bulwark against Bolshevism, the international prestige of the Polish statehood was augmented. Consequently, diplomats in London and Paris turned a deaf ear to Ukrainian requests to create a separate self-governing Ukrainian state in Eastern Galicia. The strategy of seeking to use mass non-violent contention in order to represent Polish domination in the region as illegitimate did not pay off.

In sum, *contained and transgressive contention yielded little result, because both strategies challenged well-consolidated elites that were able to repress transgressive contention and to neutralize contained contention through cunning political maneuvers*. Thus, the POS was closed for all Ukrainian nationalists and they themselves were discouraged with regards to the prospects of the Ukrainian independence. (The B2-zone represents this trend on Scheme 1.)

Soon, however, political changes sent more inspiring signals to both moderates and radicals. In 1921–22, the Polish authorities sought to decrease ethnic tensions all over the country. For this purpose, they used diplomatic backchannels to reach the West Ukrainian People's Republic government in exile. The Polish regime put a compromise on the table: political autonomy would be granted to the Ukrainian populace, on condition that Ukrainians recognize the incorporation of Galicia into the Second Polish Republic.[44] On 26 September 1922, the Sejm passed the "Bill on local self-government in the voivodeships of L'viv, Ternopil', and Stanislav," energetic objection by the Polish nationalist *Popular National Union* notwithstanding. For moderate Ukrainian forces this looked like a positive sign: an important institutional ally (the Sejm) supported the Ukrainian cause, in addition to the fact that the bill itself provoked fractionalization within the winning elite coalition. Apparently, the POS was opening and indicating that contained contention could yield positive results. Yet, on 27 November 1922, this impression proved to be deceptive: a new governmental decree made military service in the Polish army obligatory for all Galician men. This was a violation of international principles, because Galicia was administered by the League of Nations at the time, and so Warsaw had no right to impose military service upon the local population. This decree shattered the moderates' belief that inter-ethnic reconciliation was possible. The moderates' frustration became even more pronounced with the assassination of a newly elected President of Poland Gabriel Narutowicz. Narutowicz won the elections, owing to his moderate program that attracted most of the minority votes. The Polish conservative and far-right circles were distraught at the victory of an "anti-Polish candidate."[45] They obstructed and vilified Narutowicz in the media, and finally on 16 December 1922, a young extremist who had some ties with the rightist *National Democratic Party* shot the President at an art exhibition. The assassination of

---

[44] Klyment Fedevych, *Halyts'ki ukraiintsi v Pol'shchi, 1920–1939 rr*, 121.
[45] Adam Michnik, "Nenavist' stochnykh kanav," *Kontinent* 1 (2006): 174–91.

Narutowicz meant that Ukrainian moderates lost an important institutional ally. This, and the further drift of the government to the right that followed the death of Narutowicz, closed the POS for contained contention after a brief period of opening.

The same period witnessed POS fluctuation for radical Ukrainian nationalists. The newly adopted Constitution of 1921 secured land property rights for owners of great estates in the eastern regions of the Second Polish Republic. This was a blatant contravention of the First Act of 1920 that made provisions for land repartition.[46] The First Act assured the landless Ukrainian peasants who inhabited the eastern regions of the Second Polish Republic that they would have their share of land at the expense of the magnates. This policy proposal engendered some loyalty among the Ukrainian peasantry to the state they had recently fought against. The Constitution ruined both peasants' expectations and the credibility of the Polish authorities. Furthermore, the Polish nationalist winning coalition inaugurated the policy of colonization *(osadnictwo wojskowe)* in the eastern regions. Under a bill of December 1920, land shares in the territories which previously belonged to the Romanov empire (e.g. Volhynia) were granted to Polish military veterans for their service.[47] The bill antagonized local Ukrainians; not only were they deprived of the land they coveted, but they also saw land-shares given to Polish military servicemen in reward for the defeat they had inflicted on the West Ukrainian People's Republic.

The maladroit governmental policy and the peasant discontent it provoked promised new opportunities for Ukrainian radicals who sought to continue armed struggle against the Polish domination. Seasoned commanders like Yevhen Konovalets' and Andrii Mel'nyk decided to utilize covert military operations to political ends,[48] and this led them to transgressive contention. In order to

---

[46] Peter Stachura, *Poland, 1918–1945: An Interpretive and Documentary History of the Second* Republic (London: Routledge, 2004), 48–49.

[47] Janina Stobniak-Smogorzewska, *Kresowe osadnictwo wojskowe 1920-1945* (Warszawa: Instytut Studiów Politycznych, 2003), 17–23.

[48] Zynovii Knysh, "Konovalets' v ochakh molodshoii heneratsii UVO," in *Ievhen Konovalets' i ioho doba*, ed. Iurii Boyko (Munich: Vydannia Fundatsii im. Ievhena Konoval'tsia, 1974), 275.

provide contention with organizational structure, Ukrainian commanders founded the *Ukrainian Military Organization* (UVO). UVO used guerrilla warfare to galvanize popular discontent, amplify Ukrainian collective identity, and call into question the ability of the Polish administration to control the eastern regions. By the year 1922 the division within the Polish elites (made overt by the assassination of Narutowicz) and the ineptitude of the Polish security service when it came to dealing with transgressive contentious politics[49] opened the POS for the radicals. As a result, transgressive contention thrived in the year 1922: there were 38 acts of sabotage on the railway, arson attacks on arms depots in the city of Przemyśl, demolition of the telegraph communication system between L'viv and Bibrka, and attacks on police stations in towns of Iavoriv, Horodok, and Uhniv, as well as 37 armed assaults on Polish policemen and servicemen.[50]

Around this time the first cracks in the relationship between moderate and radical Ukrainian nationalists appeared. In August 1922, the radicals called for a boycott of the elections to the Sejm; the moderates deemed this unwise and refused to follow. In response, on 15 October 1922, the radicals assassinated one of the outspoken leaders of the moderate camp, Sydir Tverdohlib. The assassination and the trial of Stepan Fedak Jr. for other failed assassination attempts[51] provoked a temporary weakening of the moderates, which in turn amplified the belief that transgressive contention was the only feasible way to promote Ukrainian interests. Therefore, the

---

[49] This incompetence was illustrated during the events of September 1921, when Stepan Fedak Jr., a member of UVO and a son of a prominent Ukrainian lawyer and an ex-minister of the West Ukrainian People's Republic Stepan Fedak Sr., attempted to assassinate both Józef Piłsudski and Kazimierz Grabowski (the Lviv Voivode). The assassination failed and Fedak Jr. was detained. However, the investigators did not manage to establish that the attack had been plotted by UVO, thus the organization survived and continued its activities. Moreover, charges were pressed against activists of Ukrainian cultural revival (namely Stepan Fedak Sr., Ivan Kyveliuk (the head of *Prosvita* cultural association), Vasyl' Shchurata, and Mykhailo Halushchyns'kyi, both professors at the Lviv Clandestine Ukrainian University), which further weakened Ukrainian moderates.

[50] Anatolii Kentii, *Ukraiins'ka Viis'kova Organizatsiia v 1920-1928 rr.* (Kyiv: Instytut istorii Ukraiiny, 1998): 36.

[51] See footnote 49.

POS opened for the radicals. (The B1-zone represents this trend on the Scheme.)

The radical strategy was rooted in the belief that Poles intended "to present both the Entente powers and the Ukrainian populace with the inclusion of Galicia into Poland as a fait accompli."[52] To countervail, Ukrainian radicals sought to prove—through sabotage, boycotts, and assassinations—the inability of Poles to effectively govern the region. To their shock, on 14 March 1923, the Conference of Ambassadors of the Principal Allied and Associated Powers officially recognized Polish sovereignty over what is today L'viv, Ternopil', Rivne, Ivano-Frankivs'k, and Volhynia regions of Ukraine. The resolution proved the radical strategy to be utterly ineffective and the POS suddenly closed. The radicals were in the utmost disarray;[53] some became disillusioned with nationalist ideas altogether and joined the Communist underground.[54]

Three additional developments further complicated the resort to transgressive contention. First, the Polish security service finally adapted to UVO clandestine tactics. They penetrated the UVO organizational structure and arrested many active members of the organization. In other words, repressions were being effectively applied to block the transgressive contention. Second, a newly created Border Protection Corps (1924) all but paralyzed the vital contacts the radicals maintained with their sympathizers outside of the Second Polish Republic. There were substantial Ukrainian diasporas in Danzig, Vienna, Berlin, Prague, and Poděbrady; some of these cities served as breeding-grounds for the mobilization of foot soldiers, and others provided assistance in the form of printing propaganda materials, weapons, and money. The Border Protection Corps activities blocked access to those resources and destroyed the networks of contention, which further weakened UVO. Third, in the mid-1920s the Polish government introduced a new currency and managed to vivify the economic life. The material improvement of everyday life

---

[52] Stepan Lenkavs'kyi, *Ukraiins'kyi natsionalizm: tvory*, 66.
[53] See Lenkavs'kyi's testimony on the members' mood within UVO: Lenkavs'kyi, *Ukraiins'kyi natsionalizm*, 149.
[54] Anatoliy Kentiy, *Ukraiins'ka Viis'kova Organizatsiia v 1920-1928 rr.*, 34.

lessened the popular discontent thus decreasing the pool of local resources available to contentious actors. These three factors combined had significantly hindered the transgressive contentious politics, which explains why between 1923 and 1926 it was reduced to infrequent acts not dissimilar to petty crimes, such as bank robberies.

Therefore, *by the year 1926, after some fluctuations, the POS became firmly closed for both the contained and transgressive contention.* (The shift from the B1-zone to B2-zone represents this trend on Scheme 1.)

## 3. Sanation (1926–30)

In May 1926, the most respected military and political figure of interwar Poland, Marshal Józef Piłsudski, reacted to the nefarious combination of a prolonged governmental crisis, economic stagnation, and a reshuffling of international alliances which seemed to threaten the Polish state. The ineptitude of the ruling elites, the ineffectiveness of the republican system, and his own dislike of political party competition,[55] prompted Piłsudski to stage a coup d'état in May 1926. It brought to power many active-duty officers and other men with substantial experience of military service. Piłsudski himself was promptly elected President of State, but he ceded the post to Ignacy Mościcki, opting to rule the country from behind the throne. The new regime took a symbolic name "Sanation," for it promised to be curative for both state and society after years of parliamentary calamity.

Even though the authoritarian drift made the political regime simultaneously more repressive and less accountable, this was only partially true for Ukrainian nationalists. In fact, the rule of an ally and a good friend of Symon Petliura opened the POS for them. Not only did Piłsudski have a personal interest in the Ukrainian question (which itself provided new opportunities to contentious actors), but he also advocated considerable policy changes on this front, being

---

[55] For Piłsudski's political views see: Andrzej Garlicki, *Józef Piłsudski 1867–1935* (Lublin: Czytelnik, 1988).

an ardent proponent of the idea of a federalized Poland. In addition, he promoted the "Prometheanism doctrine," a geopolitical vision that stipulated that Polish geopolitical security was heavily dependent on the existence of a security zone between Russia and Poland, a zone composed of friendly national states, including Ukraine. Consequently, the "Prometheanism" program outlined a Polish cultural mission to promote the eventual formation of a Ukrainian state to the east of the Zbruch river.[56]

Given Piłsudski's geopolitical vision, it is only logical that his governmental team included pragmatic Ukrainophiles as Henryk Józewski and Tadeusz Hołówko, whose policies aimed to encourage the economic and cultural revival of the Ukrainian minority. Moreover, the ideological underpinning of the new regime was the so-called "solidarism principle." Solidarism sought to ensure the political loyalty of ethnic minorities through their thorough inclusion into the social structure of the Second Polish Republic.[57] This was a reversal of the assimilation policy practiced during the parliamentary period. In practical terms this meant that the Sanation regime aimed to bring Ukrainians to political dialogue and legal political participation, a process which served to significantly empower the moderate Ukrainian nationalists. They received both access to conventional politics and more effective leverage to affect the government through contained contention. Thus, the POS started opening again for the moderates.

In July 1927, Piotr Dunin-Borkowski, an outspoken partisan of the Prometheanism doctrine, assumed the highest administrative post in the L'viv Voivodeship (*Województwo lwowskie*). He implemented a policy program intended "to eliminate the objective causes of economic discontent observed among Ukrainians and to reach actors able to represent Ukrainian interests for the purpose of overcoming the separatist tendencies and building a common agenda to

---

[56] Cf.: Sergiusz Mikulicz, *Prometeizm w polityce II Rzeczypospolitej* (Warszawa: Książka i Wiedza, 1971); and Richard Woytak, "The Promethean Movement in Interwar Poland," *East European Quarterly* XVIII no. 3 (1984): 273–78.
[57] Władysław Kulesza, *Koncepcje ideowo-polityczne obozu rządzącego w Polsce w latach 1926-1935* (Wrocław: Ossolineum, 1985), 133.

tackle the most notorious challenges."⁵⁸ In December 1928, Kyiv-born Henryk Józewski, a close friend of both Józef Piłsudski and Symon Petliura, took office of the head of the Volhynian Voivodeship (*Województwo Wołyńskie*). Józewski wished to transform Volhynia into a region of mutual reconciliation and understanding between Poles and Ukrainians. To promote his vision, Józewski invited Ukrainians to participate in local management and reestablished Ukrainian as a compulsory language in schools.⁵⁹

These and other developments inspired moderate Ukrainian nationalists who welcomed the Sanation regime and its policies. As early as in November 1926, a new UNDO program was adopted, a program overtly declaring that the organization would seek cooperation with the new ruling elites. The government reciprocated by facilitating (and often funding) UNDO's organizational, financial, and mobilizational activities. Owing to this support, UNDO quickly grew to become the dominant organization of the Ukrainian minority. Cultural, economic, and political initiatives promoted by UNDO brought Ukrainian artists, businessmen, and moderate politicians closer and closer to the mainstream of the social life within the Second Polish Republic. The moderate strategy reached its highest point in 1928, when Ukrainians both voted and competed for parliamentary seats.

The radical nationalists, however, were alarmed. They suffered gravely from the opposite flank effect, because their own transgressive strategy was deemed ineffective, archaic, and purposeless by many Ukrainians. As a result, sympathizers of the Ukrainian cause opted to invest money, time, and effort in moderate activities, which shrunk the resource pool available to the radicals. Moreover, the regime espoused policy that facilitated promotion of Ukrainian interests either through conventional politics or through contained contention, severely penalizing any attempts at transgressive contention. Thus, by the end of the year 1928, the regime had the upper

---

58  Volodymyr Komar, "Ukraiins'ke pytannia v politytsi uriadiv Pol'shchi (1926–1935 rr.)," *Ukraiins'kyi istorychnyi zhurnal* 5 (2001): 122.
59  Timothy Snyder, *Sketches from a Secret War: A Polish Artist's Mission to Liberate Soviet Ukraine* (New Haven, CT: Yale University Press, 2005).

hand. It was largely invulnerable to the radicals' strategy and was constantly draining their resources by supporting the moderates. Given another two or three years, the radicals would have been utterly isolated, weakened, and eventually driven out of existence.

Between 1928 and 1929, however, the Sanation regime suffered several serious blows that undermined the regime's capacity and granted the radicals a much-needed revival. The first blow came with the Great Depression. Although the economic crisis peaked in Poland in 1935, the repercussions of economic meltdowns in the US and Germany struck the Polish economy immediately, in the late 1920s. With the financial market plummeting and the unemployment rate skyrocketing, the regime was suddenly faced with economic grievances of the population, which rapidly evolved into political dissent. Secondly, between November 1928 and March 1929, the public was outraged by a scandal involving Gabriel Czechowicz, the Minister of Finances and a close friend of Piłsudski. The media learned that Czechowicz had embezzled a large amount of money from the national treasury. With the economic crises and the scandal combined, the anti-Piłsudski opposition was suddenly reinvigorated. In June 1930, several prominent political parties held a congress in Kraków (*Centrolew – Kongres Obrony Prawa i Wolności Ludu*). The congress participants blamed Piłsudski personally for usurping power, and demanded that parliamentary democracy be restored. The regime retaliated with political repression: many prominent oppositional leaders were arrested, including the ex-Prime Minister Wincenty Witos and the hero of the Polish uprising in Silesia Wojciech Korfanty.

These events suddenly opened the POS for transgressive contention, due to a shift in perception: the radicals now saw the regime, which once seemed firm and in full control of the situation, to be corrupted and economically weak. In addition, it provoked political opposition and later arrested its leadership for obviously trumped-up charges. In other words, Ukrainian radicals believed Piłsudski's regime to be debilitated and unprotected, for they observed pervasive elite-fractioning, diminishing economic capacities, and ineffective repression. The radicals perceived and constructed new opportunities to oppose such a regime, and the POS opened.

This shift explains why the transgressive contention became intense and bold after late 1928, when the radicals provoked street fights with the police in L'viv (1 November 1928),[60] bombed the national trade fair *Targi Wschodnie* (7 September 1929),[61] and organized more than two thousand episodes of transgressive contentious actions. UVO became present in the political process of the Second Polish Republic and even launched its newest project, the Organization of Ukrainian Nationalists, due to the opening of the POS in the late 1920s.

To summarize, *in 1926–30 the dismantling of the parliamentary republic and installation of the Sanation regime made the POS open for both moderate and radical Ukrainian nationalists.* (The D-zone and the highest inflection point of the inverted U-curve illustrate this period on Scheme 1.)

### 4. Pacification and Normalization (1930–38)

Pacification policy, that is, the retaliatory acts by Polish authorities against the Ukrainian populace used in order to inhibit its participation in political contention, have been described quite thoroughly in Ukrainian historical studies, and so there is little need to reiterate the key events here.[62] Rather, I argue that pacification policy itself should be placed within the broader context of the general repressive turn of the regime as it faced challenges posed by political opposition in the 1930s. Likewise, both the quest for and the policy of normalization—an attempt to find a viable political solution for the "Ukrainian" question taken by UNDO in 1935–38—were the outcomes of the general political dynamics rather than ends in their own right.

---

[60] Mykola Klymyshyn, *V pokhodi do voli*, t. 1 (Detroit: Ukraiins'ka knyharnia, 1975), 262.

[61] Petro Mirchuk, *Narys istorii Orhanizatsii Ukraiins'kykh Natsionalistiv* (Munich: Ukraiinske Vydavnytstvo, 1968), 215.

[62] For details see Andrzej Chojnowski, *Koncepcje polityki narodowościowej rządów polskich w latach 1921–1939* (Wrocław: Ossolineum, 1979): 155–160, 173–181; Wysocki, *Organizacja Ukraińskich Nacjonalistów*, 128–34; and Roman Skakun, *Patsyfikatsiia* (Lviv: Ukrainian Catholic University Press, 2012).

No sooner had the Polish political opposition challenged both the legitimacy and the supremacy of Piłsudski than the authorities retaliated by instituting further restraints on the remnant democratic procedures, together with political repression. There were undeniable signs that the regime was drifting further towards a full-fledged dictatorship: military and security officers attained new governmental offices, a new "April" Constitution, which significantly increased power to the executive branch and dismantled the checks-and-balances system, was adopted, civic activities were scrutinized and—if loyalty to the regime lacked—suppressed, as it was with the notorious case of fifty university professors who lost their jobs in 1932 because they leaned towards the opposition.[63] In their efforts to regulate the dissent, the authorities often resorted to rather dubious practices, such as paying thugs to violently disperse oppositional mass rallies, and carrying out extrajudicial incarcerations. In July 1934, Prime Minister Leon Kozłowski suggested and President Ignacy Mościcki sanctioned the establishment of a concentration camp at Bereza Kartuska. Bereza Kartuska's inmates were predominantly political prisoners, namely the Polish communists (estimated to have composed up to a half of all detainees[64]); socialists; leaders of a peasants' party (*Stronnictwo Ludowe*) that encouraged Polish peasants to challenge the authorities; members of the far-right groups (e.g. *Obóz Narodowo-Radykalny*); and leaders of national minority organizations,[65] including radical Ukrainian nationalists.

Given the overarching regime's strategy to brutally suppress any political dissent, many notorious cases (detentions of the prominent Ukrainian community leaders like Dmytro Paliiv, Volodymyr Tselevych, and Osyp Kohut; banishment of the Scouting organization "Plast"; harassment of cultural unions like "Enlightenment," "Native School," "Family"; let alone reprisals in rural areas and extrajudicial summary executions) represented not an anti-Ukrainian

---

[63] Stachura, *Poland, 1918–1945*, 67.
[64] Andrzej Garlicki, "Bereza, polski obóz koncentracyjny," *Gazeta Wyborcza*, 19–20 April 2008, http://wyborcza.pl/1,76842,5134208.html?disableRedirects=true (accessed 10 November 2016).
[65] Wojciech Śleszyński, *Obóz odosobnienia w Berezie Kartuskiej: 1934–1939* (Białystok: Dom Wydawniczy Benkowski, 2003).

policy, but rather the establishment of a generally repressive political system. Therefore, *in 1930–35 POS was closing for all types of contentious politics*. (The shift from D-zone to the C-zone illustrates this trend on Scheme 1.)

The pressure exerted by the regime forced the moderates to look for a mutually convenient regulation, which in turn begat the normalization policy. To be more precise, the moderates now publicly declared their willingness to relaunch a dialogue with the authorities in order to obtain at least some means of promoting the Ukrainian minority's interests.

There was an international component of the disparate quest for normalization. In 1934, the German–Polish Non-Aggression Pact was signed. The document ostensibly securitized the western borders of the Second Polish Republic, thus reinforcing the Piłsudski regime vis-à-vis Ukrainian nationalists by decreasing the German support for Ukrainians. Moreover, in the mid-1930s the Ukrainian minority of the Second Polish Republic learned about persecutions of the Ukrainian intelligentsia and man-made famine (*Holodomor*) in the Soviet Union. This knowledge led to a decrease in pro-Soviet attitudes among Ukrainians in Poland, which made any political orientation toward the USSR non-viable.[66] Having lost possible international allies, the moderate camp had little choice but to look for normalization with the regime.

The political leadership of the Second Polish Republic had their own reasons to renew cooperation with moderate Ukrainian nationalists due to internal pressure. The charismatic ruler Piłsudski died in office in May 1935. The next parliamentary elections were scheduled for the fall of 1935, but the Polish opposition threatened to boycott them. These developments made the erosion of public support and the lack of political legitimacy the most pressing challenges for the Sanation regime. Still, there was a possibility that the cloak of legitimacy and the popular mandate could be obtained, oppositional boycott notwithstanding, were the regime to involve representatives of ethnic minorities in the political process in general and in the elections of 1935 in particular. The ruling elites decided

---

[66] Chojnowski, *Koncepcje polityki narodowościowej*, 176–205.

to play this card, making reconciliation with the Ukrainian moderate camp necessary.

As an initial step towards normalization the regime demanded active participation of Ukrainians in the elections. The demand was granted, although the overall electoral turnout of 1935 proved to be the lowest in the history of the Second Polish Republic. Next, UNDO, which managed to bring several of its members to parliament, supported governmental initiatives with votes. In return, the Ukrainians demanded policy concessions, namely: halting the Polish colonization of the regions inhabited by Ukrainians; inaugurating a Ukrainian university (a constant governmental promise since the 1920s); promoting usage of the Ukrainian language; and subsidizing Ukrainian cultural initiatives.

None of these demands were satisfied. The regime failed to keep most of the promises it had previously made in order to engage the Ukrainian moderates in cooperation. For instance, although Prime Minister Marian Zyndram-Koscialkowski pledged to halt the colonization policy, since, as historian Ivan Kedryn puts it, "he himself saw that the eastern regions were overpopulated and Ukrainian villages were stricken by land hunger, not only had the situation failed to improve, but it had also deteriorated, because Minister [of Agriculture] Juliusz Poniatowski made land reparation for the Ukrainian peasantry all but impossible."[67] Likewise, contrary to all promises, the regime amplified repressions against Ukrainian philanthropic societies: it banned charity donations to support "Native school," prohibited commemoration of the 70-year anniversary of "Enlightenment," and made several attempts to outlaw the "Meadow" (*Luh*) sport association. The symbolically important problem of Polonization at elementary schools was ignored. Another significant question for the Ukrainian minority was the internal border (the so-called "Sokal border") that separated Galicia and Volhynia and constrained freedom of transportation between the two most Ukrainian-populated regions. The Polish administration (including Henryk Józewski) erected (around the year of 1925) the Sokal border in order to shield Volhynia from nationalist ideas

---

[67] Ivan Kedryn, *Zhyttia, podii, liudy* (New York: Chervona Kalyna, 1976), 256.

penetrating from Galicia; however, humiliating procedures of border control antagonized Ukrainians even further.

But the single most devastating policy that effectively doomed the normalization was revindication of ecclesiastical lands. The reason for this policy was a particular ethno-confessional division especially pronounced in Volhynia and Chełm Land: as a rule, Orthodox Christians were Ukrainians, whereas Catholics were Poles. The regime decided to tackle the Ukrainian question in the region by decreasing the number of Orthodox Christians. To attain this goal the authorities took the land from Orthodox churches and gave it to the Catholic ones. Revindication policy as a strategy to diminish the Ukrainian presence in Volhynia and Chełm Land had been espoused by the leaders of the Second Polish Republic since the 1920s,[68] but it grew in scope and became more brutal after December 1935 when the Committee for National Questions adopted a more vigorous policy line. In practical terms this policy led not only to eviction of the Orthodox priests from the regions, but also to demolition of Orthodox places of worship.[69]

Given the circumstances, the head of UNDO Vasyl Mudryi declared the normalization policy utterly ineffective in December 1938. This represented an overt recognition that both conventional politics and contained contention were of little use when it came to promoting Ukrainian interests in the Second Polish Republic.

**Catalytic Mobilization**

The failure to achieve any substantial Polish–Ukrainian reconciliation was affected by the transgressive contention aptly and ruthlessly utilized by the radical Ukrainian nationalists in the 1930s. The historiography recounting the Ukrainian transgressive contention

---

[68] Mirosława Papierzyńska-Turek, *Między tradycją a rzeczywistością: państwo wobec prawosławia 1918–1939* (Warszawa: Państwowe Wydawnictwo Naukowe, 1989), 359.

[69] Bohdan Hud', "Polityka 'revindykatsii' na Kholmshchyni ta Volyni 1937-1938 rr. ta ii naslidky dlia ukraiins'ko-pol'skykh stosunkiv," in *Ukraiina: zbirnyk naukovykh prats'* 21 (2012), 259.

during this period is vast.⁷⁰ Suffice it to cite the boldest actions on this front: in 1931 radicals assassinated a vocal proponent of Prometheanism, Tadeusz Hołówko; in 1932 they murdered L'viv chief police officer Emilian Czechowski; in 1933 they killed the Secretary of the Soviet consulate in L'viv (and OGPU agent) Aleksei Mailov; and in 1934 the radicals assassinated Interior Minister Bronisław Pieracki.

Facing such resolute radicalism, the political leadership of the Second Polish Republic grew convinced that it was impossible to achieve any reconciliation with Ukrainian nationalists. In response, the authorities opted for forced assimilation of the Ukrainian minority, with the aim of eradicating the grass-roots support for the contentious politics. As a result, the national minorities policy espoused by the political leadership in the 1930s was similar to the program of the extreme right National Democracy (*Endecja*) movement of the 1920s. Piłsudski's integration vision converged with and was substituted by that of assimilation, always dear to his arch-rival Dmowski. This historical evolution, however, might conceal an important theoretical problem: *since the political leadership of the Second Polish Republic adopted a hardline policy against all Ukrainian nationalists in the 1930s, should this not have provoked POS closure for the radicals?* And if the POS was really closing in the 1930s, why was it the case that the transgressive contention did not become less intense during this period? Why were the radicals not forced into compliance?

All the POS indicators I discussed earlier suggest that the POS was in fact closing: the regime had undergone an authoritarian drift, the repression became harsher, the ruling elites were consolidated in their vision of how to resolve the Ukrainian question, and the transgressive contention actors had no institutional allies.

---

70   See: *Polityčhnyi teror i teroryzm v Ukraiini XIX–XX st.*, ed. Volodymyr Smolii (Kyiv: Naukova dumka, 2002); Ievhen Konovalets', *Ia biu u dzvin, aby zrushyty spravu OUN z mertvoii tochky* (Kyiv: Tempora, 2003); Anatolii Kentii, *Zbroinyi chyn ukraiins'kykh natsionalistiv* (Kyiv: Tsentral'nyi derzhavnyi arkhiv hromads'kykh orhanizatsii, 2005); Mykola Posivnych, "Ekspropriatsiina diial'nist OUN," *Vyzvol'nyi shliakh* 4 (2005): 96–103; and Petro Mirchuk, *Narys istorii OUN, 1920–1939* (Kyiv: Tsentr Doslidzhennia Vyzvol'noho Rukhu, 2007).

Nevertheless, transgressive contention persisted, and in fact grew bolder, and was ultimately never quelled by the Second Polish Republic. Thus, despite all odds the POS was somehow opening for the radicals during the 1930s. I argue that an important mechanism of *catalytic mobilization* played the decisive role in this change. Owing to this mechanism, all efforts to inhibit resource mobilization provoked backlash and multiplied the availability of resources for a given contentious actor. In other words, when catalytic mobilization occurs, contentious actors become invulnerable to the regime's counter-strategy and they can intensify their contentious politics repressions or any other strategies by the regime regardless. (The E-curve, which changes its inflection angle in response to governmental policies but goes upwards, represents the outcomes of catalytic mobilization on Scheme 1.)

I argue that catalytic mobilization is a rare mechanism. It occurs only under three concurrent conditions: contentious actors provide accurate prognoses; they can successfully replenish lost resources; and they effectively surmount the opposite flank effect. The radical Ukrainian nationalist managed to meet all three conditions, which explains why they persevered in their competition with the regime.

*Accurate prognoses* relate to the POS interpretational dimension. As David Meyer and Deborah Minkoff have suggested, contentious actors "appear more likely to respond positively to relatively predictable changes in the political system."[71] It is equally conceivable that in situations when political leadership acts according to the expectations and prognoses of contentious actors, they would understand the events as positive cues. Hence, the POS—the ideas about what is feasible and effective under the given circumstances—will open.

This was the case of radical Ukrainian nationalists under the Second Polish Republic. Since the military destruction of the West Ukrainian People's Republic and the forceful inclusion of Galicia into the Polish state, Ukrainian radicals tried to intensify the ethno-

---

[71] David Meyer and Deborah Minkoff, "Conceptualizing Political Opportunity," *Social Forces* 82 no. 4 (2004): 1478.

political conflict between Poles and Ukrainians. With the regime becoming more authoritarian and persecutions against Ukrainians constantly increasing, the situation perfectly coincided with the radicals' prognoses. They were convinced—and tried to persuade anyone who would listen—that Poles had imposed imperialist and chauvinist domination over Ukrainians, and that this domination was totally illegitimate and enforced only by brutal coercion. Emergency courts, roundups, destruction of Orthodox churches, and compulsory Polonization in schools mostly corroborated this vision. Consequently, the second part of the radical argument—that the imperialist domination should be overthrown by violence—also seemed largely substantiated. As for the radicals themselves, the more repressive the regime tended to be, the more accurate their prognosis appeared. They understood repressions and persecutions as signs that their strategy was ultimately correct; in response, they attacked Polish colonists and politicians ever more resolutely.

*Resource replenishment* depends on effective organizational structure: if contention entrepreneurs are capable of (1) establishing several separate breeding-grounds; (2) finding a safe-haven abroad; (3) effectuating logistic management that helps to cover losses in one sector by transferring resources from another one; and (4) capitalizing on available cultural resources (identity, ethnicity, collective emotions), then the regime's repression will be tolerable. When contentious actors survive repressions and persevere, they deem the regime to be a feeble opponent; thus their expectations of winning increase, and the POS opens.

The radical Ukrainian nationalists managed to make the Ukrainian public ever more sensitive to cultural issues. This was an important step that constituted a pool of sympathizers. Next, they diffused their radical vision not only in the Galician foothold but also in other Ukrainian territories, which until the late 1920s remained less radicalized. Finally, the radicals penetrated student circles in Danzig, Prague, and Poděbrady, which provided them with much-needed safe-havens. The salutary outcomes of these efforts became apparent in the mid-1930s, when all of the OUN Regional Leadership (including Stepan Bandera, Mykola Lebid, Iaroslav Karpynets) had been detained, but the organization mobilized and promoted new activists (like Lev Rebet and Oleksandr Hasyn) both at home and abroad, and eventually survived the decimation.

*The opposite flank effect* is overcome when a contentious faction successfully persuades the pool of sympathizers that the competing faction's strategy is futile. This is the third component for the catalytic mobilization. With the radical flank effect no longer in action, a victorious contentious actor appropriates all available resources which it used to share with the rival faction. This provokes a considerable influx in resources, which in turn provides new opportunities to diversify contentious performances, tackle the regime from several angles, and build more stable inter-organizational alliances; thus, it opens the POS.

There are different ways to surmount the radical flank effect. One faction can annihilate the other by force; it can capitalize on the regime's repressive actions that have temporally weakened its rival; or the two factions can overcome their differences and reunite against the regime. In the Ukrainian case, the opposite flank effect had been eventually surmounted due to inaccurate predictions by the moderates which discouraged and alienated their supporters. There were solid reasons for such loss of hope. Despite a governmental team composed of pragmatic Ukrainophiles and deliberate steps taken by the moderates to promote Ukrainian interests by legal means, the moderates themselves were eventually faced with repression and forceful assimilation. Thus, they lost their faith. The memoirs of a convinced partisan of Polish–Ukrainian reconciliation are revealing in this respect: "When all [the efforts to reconcile two ethnicities] failed, it is uniquely the Polish part which is to be blamed, for it had rarely showed a modicum of good will… Both the authorities and the Polish press reiterated that we should live together, but since 1918 they themselves through their actions *were constantly reproducing the mood of war*" (emphasis added—IG).[72] This extract is revealing not because it contains a rather harsh and unilateral condemnation of the Polish side, but rather because the author, a prominent moderate, bluntly admits that a constant war was being waged between Ukrainians and Poles in the Second Polish

---

[72] Kedryn, *Zhyttia, podii, liudy*, 247.

Republic, that the two ethnicities could not peacefully coexist within a single state. The competition between moderate and radical Ukrainian nationalists had petered out by the late 1930s, because the POS finally closed for the moderates who themselves lost all faith in the effectiveness of contained transgression.

With the moderate option off the table, people who had any nationalist ideals gravitated closer towards the radicals. After all, the radicals had a well-built organizational structure; the radical interpretation of the nature of Polish–Ukrainian affairs seemed to be compelling; and the radicals had a set of solutions and clear program of action regarding how to resolve the Ukrainian question on Ukrainian terms. Thus, the conceptual horizon for any Ukrainian-minded patriot was all but closed: there was no other viable alternative to transgressive contentious politics. This gave a final thrust to catalytic mobilization.

The radicals skillfully used newly available resources to play on the mistakes and blunders of the Polish authorities in order to maximize their radical goals. The famous "Volhynian experiment" by Henryk Józewski is revealing in this respect. It is true that his gubernatorial policy, which aimed to promote peaceful co-existence of the two ethnicities within the same voivodeship, yielded little results.[73] However, this evaluation of Józewski's initiatives should be nuanced: his policy failed to bring the moderates' vision to fruition, but it vastly facilitated the accomplishment of radicals' plans, for they benefited from Józewski's pro-Ukrainian policy to take foothold within the Volhynian society. As Timothy Snyder put it, the radicals:

> easily penetrated the non-governmental organizations Józewski sponsored, and exploited the relative freedom of Volhynia. They were not satisfied by Józewski's limited reforms, and promised peasants more freedom and more land. Once again, attempts at federalism were easily undermined by these issues. If Volhynia was to enjoy land reform, why import thousands of Polish

---

[73] Hans-Jorg Bömelburg, "Die polnisch-ukrainischen Beziehungen 1922–1939," *Jahrbücher für Geschichte Osteuropas* 39, no. 1 (1991): 92.

officers as colonists? If Ukrainian was to be taught in schools, why not create entirely Ukrainian schools?[74]

I argue that the radicals managed to break the Sokal border and to take root in Volhynia due to the regional authorities' policy which effectively swung the regional POS open. This made Volhynia an ample pool of resources. Because of the abundance of resources, Volhynia evolved from a secondary stage (as compared to Galicia) into a laboratory of ideas and tactics. Throughout the year of 1943, this evolution would come to yield the most ominous outcomes.

---

[74] Timothy Snyder, "Federalism and Nationalism in Polish Eastern Policy," *Journal of International Affairs* 111 (2003): 115.

# Allies or Collaborators? The Organization of Ukrainian Nationalists and Nazi Germany during the Occupation of Ukraine in 1941–43

Igor Barinov

***Abstract:*** *The question of how to classify the relationship between the Organization of Ukrainian Nationalists (OUN) and Nazi Germany during World War II is both extremely complex from the scholarly point of view, and heavily politicized and emotionally charged. Was the OUN's relationship to Nazi Germany a case of a full-fledged alliance, or should we rather view this as an instance of collaboration, in which the OUN was in a subordinate position vis-à-vis the Nazi authorities? This article sets out to classify the relations between the Ukrainian nationalists and various structures of the German Reich during the different periods of their cooperation, with a particular focus on the period of the Nazi occupation of Ukraine. The specificity of the OUN case, especially when it comes to this particular period, means that the OUN's actions do not fit neatly within a clear-cut ally/collaborator dichotomy. In this article, a case is made for viewing this relationship as neither an alliance nor collaboration, but rather a specific form of situational tactical cooperation arising out of conditions in which the aims and intentions of the two parties were in temporary alignment with one another. In making this argument, the article seeks to contribute to the scholarship on the problem of how to define collaboration in the context of the particular conditions of the Eastern front.*

The activities of the Organization of Ukrainian Nationalists (OUN) during World War II have long been the subject of intense, and often deeply politicized, academic debate.[1] It would be no exaggeration to claim, as Ukrainian researcher Yana Primachenko has done, that the wartime activities of the OUN and its Banderite wing are "among the most controversial and politically motivated topics in the modern historical discourse of Central Eastern Europe."[2] This is a topic that also has urgent relevance in contemporary Ukraine. The OUN's key motto—"nation above all" (*natsiya ponad use*)—has proved attractive for Ukrainian nationalists today. It has taken on new life in the context of the ongoing armed conflict in Eastern Ukraine, which, in the eyes of nationalists, not only disrupts the country's unity and sovereignty, but also threatens the very existence of the Ukrainian nation as such. The strength of this idea's emotional charge can serve to disable reflection about the risks with which it is fraught.[3] In this article I begin by setting out to clarify the most complex issues in the relationship between Nazis and different groups of Ukrainian nationalists in occupied Ukraine. Next, I suggest how they can be classified and understood in the particular conditions of war and occupation. Finally, I evaluate the perception of these events in the mass consciousness in modern Ukraine.

**The OUN and Nazi Germany on the Eve of the Invasion of the Soviet Union**

The Organization of Ukrainian Nationalists is often demonized as a menacing monolithic force, and yet in fact it was never characterized by internal unity. From its emergence in 1929, two main power

---

[1] Similarly intense debate has surrounded the historiography on the biographies of the OUN's leaders, with the discussion over Grzegorz Rossoliński-Liebe's biography of Stepan Bandera a case in point; Grzegorz Rossoliński-Liebe, *Stepan Bandera: The Life and Afterlife of a Ukrainian Nationalist: Fascism, Genocide, and Cult* (Stuttgart: ibidem-Verlag, 2014).

[2] Yana Primachenko, "Evoliutsiia natsional'nogo voprosa v ideologii OUN(b) v gody Vtoroi mirovoi voiny," in *Sovetskie natsii i natsional'naia politika v 1920-1950-e gody*, ed. N. Volynchik (Moskva: Rosspen, 2013), 396.

[3] These risks have been evaluated by Aleksei Miller in his latest work *Natsiia, ili mogushchestvo mifa* (Sankt-Petersburg: EU Press, 2016), 130ff.

centers were apparent—in the diaspora, and in Galicia. The former was headed by ex-members of the Ukrainian Military Organization (*Ukraiins'ka Viis'kova Organizatsiia*—UVO). This organization was established in Prague by veterans of the Ukrainian military formations of 1914–20. These included Yevhen Konovalets', the first leader of the OUN, and his closest associate and relative Andrii Mel'nyk, as well as Mykola Stsibors'kyi and Omelian Senyk, figures who were no less famous in the nationalistic circles of the time.

The opposite pole was represented by the regional executive committee (*ekzekutyva*) in Galicia, a group with a very different profile. Here the OUN consisted primarily of young people who had been socialized in the conditions of the existentially alien Polish state. Moreover, representatives of that generation had grown up in an atmosphere of never-ceasing violence, starting with World War I and ending with Piłsudski's "pacification" policy. It is no wonder that it was this part of Ukrainian nationalists that turned out to be the most receptive to the key points of "integral nationalism" which implied, among other things, the cult of war and violence.[4] It was the regional executive that was connected to the most famous OUN actions of the interbellum period, such as the assassinations of the secretary of the Soviet council in L'viv[5] Aleksei Maylov (1933) and the Polish Minister of the Interior Bronisław Pieracki (1934). Behind both actions were the leader of the regional line of the OUN, Stepan Bandera (aged 21 in 1933), and the head of the combative executive office (*referentura*) of the executive, Roman Shukhevych (aged 26).

Conflict between the semi-autonomous Galician regional executive and the émigré OUN leadership started quite soon and later developed into a hidden internal struggle.[6] This low-grade infighting continued for the entire 1930s and started to grow worse after the assassination of the organization leader Yevhen Konovalets' as the result of a special operation conducted by the Soviet People's Commissariat for Internal Affairs (NKVD) in 1938. In

---

[4] Kas'ianov, *Do pytannia pro ideolohiiu OUN*, 7.
[5] In this article, I will use the English spelling of the Ukrainian "L'viv" throughout, for the sake of simplicity, so as to avoid confusing the different official names of the city such as Lwów, L'vov, and Lemberg.
[6] Kas'ianov, *Do pytannia pro ideolohiiu OUN*, 4.

early 1940, it culminated in a rupture, conditioned, according to Ukrainian historian Heorhii Kas'ianov, by the problem of "center–region" relations rather than ideology.[7] Thus, two fractions emerged: the OUN-M, which adhered to the previously elected head of the organization Andrii Mel'nyk, and the so-called "revolutionary OUN," later renamed OUN-B after Stepan Bandera. The resulting state of affairs was recorded at the 2nd Extraordinary OUN Congress in Kraków in April 1941.

By this time, it had become obvious to both fractions that a future clash between Nazi Germany and the USSR was inevitable. Moreover, there was no doubt as to which side the OUN would take in the upcoming war. However, several burning issues were unresolved—what would the role of the Ukrainian nationalists be in the crusade against the Bolsheviks? What precise form would the OUN's relations with the Reich take? Finally, how would the goals of the Germans correlate with those of the Ukrainian "national revolution"?

Primarily, Ukrainian nationalists were concerned about political issues, more precisely—about the future Ukrainian statehood. The leaders of both OUN fractions based their calculations on two key points. First, relations with the Nazis would be strengthened by the similarity of their ideologies. It was not a coincidence, as Rossoliński-Liebe puts it, that in 1940–41 the OUN moved to take up numerous "rituals, symbols and propaganda methods" from European fascist movements, including extreme anti-communism and admiration for "blood and soil."[8] It was in this context that the OUN came to view the Ukrainian state (*ukrains'ka derzhava*) as a "state of/for Ukrainians," just the terms *deutsches/großdeutsches Reich* can be understood as referring to "a state of/for ethnic Germans."

Second, we find here the emergence of a notion that Ukraine occupied a special geopolitical location, and that consequently German leaders had consistently taken a particular interest in Ukraine. There is some truth in this, although, as Frank Golczewski rightly

---

[7] Kas'ianov, *Do pytannia pro ideologiiu OUN*, 17.
[8] Grzegorz Rossoliński-Liebe, "The 'Ukrainian National Revolution' of 1941: Discourse and Practice of a Fascist Movement," *Kritika* 12, no. 1 (2011): 86.

points out, the notion of a continuous German interest in Ukraine was also a product of the phantasy of Ukrainian nationalists.[9] In any case, the only person who could have answered this question about the future of the Ukrainian state was Adolf Hitler.

It has been argued in the scholarly literature that the Führer was certain from the very beginning that the existence of independent Ukraine in any form was an impossibility.[10] However, this is not the whole truth. The inconsistency of Hitler's position lay in the fact that while he was aware of Eastern European issues, he tended to fluctuate on these issues from categoricity to compliancy and back again. As the chief of the Army High Command Franz Halder stated in his diaries, in May 1941 the party ideologist Alfred Rosenberg, famous for his sympathetic attitude towards the Ukrainian nationalists, presented the Führer with a special memorandum concerning the future conception of German policy in the East, proposing to divide the territory of the USSR into a number of dependent territories and to delegate autonomy to several regions, among them Ukraine.[11] As reported by Halder, Hitler, after some hesitation,[12] turned down Rosenberg's suggestion, stating that it was only possible to include all the occupied Eastern territories in the Reich.

Most certainly Ukrainian nationalists were not aware of these discussions. One way or another, the OUN fraction leaders considered themselves as the Reich's allies, with the only difference that Melnyk recognized Germany's superiority, while Bandera insisted on a relationship of equals. Both cases were rooted in the objective conditions at the time: Mel'nyk, due to his current position, could have only expected Berlin's patronage, while Bandera had a solid basis among the population of Western Ukraine, which, by the way,

---

9   Frank Golczewski, *Deutsche und Ukrainer, 1914-1939* (Paderborn: Schöningh, 2010), 40.
10  Ryczard Torzecki, *Kwestia ukraińska w polityce III Rzeczy (1933-1945)* (Warszawa: Książka i wiedza, 1972), 172.
11  Gunther Friedrich, *Kollaboration in der Ukraine im Zweiten Weltkrieg: Die Rolle der einheimischen Stadtverwaltung während der deutschen Besetzung Charkows 1941 bis 1943*. Ph.D. Diss (Bochum, 2008), 43.
12  Q.v.: Klaus Jochen Arnold, *Die Wehrmacht und die Besatzungspolitik in den besetzten Gebieten der Sowjetunion: Kriegführung und Radikalisierung im "Unternehmen Barbarossa"* (Berlin: Duncker & Humblot, 2005), 86.

was raising numerous concerns for the NKVD during the first short period of the Soviet dominance in Western Ukraine.[13]

It is anyone's guess how the leaders of the Reich imagined their relationship with Mel'nyk and Bandera. On the one hand, the OUN-M, with its initial subordinate position, had more credibility. As early as in September 1940, Rosenberg's deputy Arno Schickedanz stressed in a letter to the Reich Main Security Office head Reinhard Heydrich, obviously having in mind the OUN-B, that the group had no claim to political independence because it was "a small homegrown terroristic organization in Galicia." According to Schickedanz, any attempt to give it such importance would be "pointless and silly."[14] Nevertheless, the *Nachtigall* ("Nightingale") battalion, formed by the Abwehr in Neuhammer (Lower Silesia) in winter 1940/41 from former Polish army officers of Ukrainian descent with good combat skills,[15] was subsequently transferred to the command of the OUN-B activist Roman Shukhevych.

It is possible that Nazi policy on this issue involved two simultaneous nominal lines of interaction with Ukrainian nationalists. The first of these, the "Rosenberg line" allowed the option of Ukrainian autonomy being granted within the framework of collaboration with the OUN in general. The second, "secret service line," planned to use the guerrilla experience of Ukrainian radicals—it was no coincidence that the the OUN-B was supervised by the secret service rather than the army or political leaders.[16] It is also indicative that an Abwehr liaison officer, Hans Koch, native of Galicia,[17] was present at the proclamation of the Ukrainian state by the OUN-B leaders in L'viv on 30 June 1941.

Therefore, by the beginning of Operation Barbarossa the answer to the first key question had been given, one way or another:

---

[13] Q.v., for instance, Andrei Artizov (ed.), *Ukrainskie natsionalisticheskie organizatsii v gody Vtoroi mirovoi voiny*, vol. 1 (Moscow: ROSSPEN, 2012), 243–51.
[14] Volodymyr Kosyk (ed.), *Das Dritte Reich und die ukrainische Frage. Dokumente 1934-1944* (München: Ukrainisches Institut, 1985), 51.
[15] Torzecki, *Kwestia ukraińska*, 204.
[16] Ivan Dereiko, *Mistsevi formuvannia nimets'koii armii ta politsii u Raikhskomisariati "Ukraina" (1941–1944 roky)* (Kyiv: Instytut istorii Ukrainy, 2012), 21.
[17] Another liaison officer who cooperated with the OUN, Alfred Bisanz, also descended from a Galician German family.

Berlin was not against the OUN's participation in the war against the USSR. But meanwhile, two other critical issues remained unresolved. The OUN's status in its relationship with Germany was not clearly defined, and no distinction seems to have been drawn by the Germans between the ambitions and goals of the OUN's two competing fractions. The question of the possible establishment of a Ukrainian state "on the liberated territory" was also unanswered. A similar neglect of these issues disabled the initial strategy during the occupation of Ukraine.

## The OUN's Collaboration with the Nazis: Interpretive Challenges

The phenomenon of collaborationism on Nazi-occupied Soviet territory is one of the most complex and contradictory topics in the history of the German–Soviet War. For Nazi Germany, which in the short period from spring 1939 and to spring 1941 spread its supremacy over the larger territory of continental Europe, the whole point of the "New Order" was understood as subordination of the capacities of the occupied states to the economic and strategic interests of the Reich. At the same time, the approach to fulfilling the occupation policies in the West and in the East was fundamentally different.

This difference was determined not only and not so much by the aims of "coercion of the Slavs" or the eschatological "struggle against Jewish Bolshevism." The Nazi notion of Eastern Europe (including Ukraine) grew out of intangible, even metaphysical categories, generated by a combination of philosophical positivism and political conservatism dating back to the concepts accepted in the Kaiserreich. One of the main elements of this idea was the so-called *"Ost"*—a specific anthropological entity, which in fact had little to do with geography and was primarily used to separate the "Eastern barbarians" from the *Kulturboden*, lands deemed to be part of the "true civilization," structured by Germans.

It is important to note that the Nazis vewed the European countries occupied at the beginning of the war (e.g. Denmark and France) as having already been an integral part of *Kulturboden;* the

*Ost*, by contrast, had yet to be "discovered." The real encounter with lands and peoples in the East, which often turned out to be traumatic in contrast to the Nazi geopolitical fantasies, caused a sharp dissonance and exposed the destructive potential hidden in this conservative phenomenology. During the war the full brunt of this destructive potential was felt in Poland, Belarus, and Ukraine.

On the other hand, mental and political features also played a role. Thus, for example, the Protectorate of Bohemia and Moravia, as well as quasi-independent Slovakia and Croatia, emerged on the territory controlled by the Nazi Reich. It is difficult to judge whether such "goodwill" was the result of Hitler's nostalgia (at the time of his youth in Austria these lands were part of the Habsburg Empire). In any event, these (pseudo)state entities, although considered to be Slavic, were conditionally treated by the Nazis as "cultivated," since they had historically been in close contact with the Germans.

Ukraine featured little within this system of thought. From the Nazi perspective, the greater part of the Ukrainian SSR had already been a part of the "Soviet Judea," which meant that its population had undergone a deeper "bolshevization" than peoples living elsewhere in Eastern Europe. In this regard, the remark of Roman Il'nyts'kyi, a fellow campaigner of Stets'ko and Bandera and prominent historian of the OUN, that Ukraine and Russia "were just the same for Hitler,"[18] is not far from the truth. It is quite symptomatic that in the official German correspondence Ukrainians, seemingly familiar to the Germans at least from the time of World War I, were called "Ruthenians,"[19] as in Austria-Hungary, or even "Russians,"[20] insofar as they were Soviet citizens. Moreover, as Alfred Rosenberg stressed in his memoirs, Hitler was intensely frustrated by the failed attempt of the Germans to "discover" Ukraine and to "involve" it in the "cultural world" during the occupation of 1918, to which the

---

[18] Roman Ilnytzkyj, *Deutschland und die Ukraine 1934-1945: Tatsachen europäischer Ostpolitik* (München: Osteuropa-Institut, 1955), 26, 129.
[19] Russian State Military Archive (RGVA), f. 1370k, op. 1, d. 10, l. 246.
[20] State Archive of the Russian Federation (GARF), f. R7021, op. 148, d. 219, l. 1.

Ukrainians had responded by killing the Kaiser's viceroy, General Eichhorn.²¹

For most Soviet Ukrainians, Germany likewise remained *terra incognita*. The older generation recalled the "Germans of the Kaiser" and the times of the previous occupation. The young generation at best might have met "Rotfront" activists during the Soviet industrialization, but in general imagined Germans by means of school textbooks and the official press. The logical disorientation of people overtaken in the occupied territory was exacerbated by the fact, that in a short period of time (from June 1939 to June 1941) the Soviet authorities and, accordingly, the state propaganda changed position drastically three times—the Germans were first identified as "Fascists;" then as "strategic Allies;" and then "Fascists" once again. This unsurprisingly brought confusion to the minds and souls of even loyal Soviet citizens.²²

Many photographs taken in the different regions of Ukraine in the first weeks and months of occupation prove that the local population met the Germans with a mixture of hospitality and uncertainty. Yet a positive attitude to the invaders need not always reflect joy at being liberated from the "Soviet tyranny;" it could also be the result of a lack of understanding of how to behave under the new conditions. This is the complicated context in which the activities of both local residents and Ukrainian nationalists should be evaluated.

The historian researching this issue immediately faces the problem of how to define the terms "collaborator" and "collaborationist."²³ Often the term "collaborationist" is used in the literature to denote as least two fundamentally different phenomena—

---

21  Alfred Rosenberg, *Letzte Aufzeichnungen: Ideale und Idole der nationalsozialistischen Revolution* (Göttingen: Plesse-Verlag, 1955), 214.
22  Vasilii Kulikov, *Okkupatsiia Vinnitsy (18.07.1941 - 20.03.1944): svidetel'stvo ochevidtsa* (Kyiv: Parapan, 2012), 84f.
23  The issue of defining collaboration on the occupied Soviet territory has been articulated by Oleg Budnitskii, q.v. Oleg Budnitskii (ed.), *Svershilos'—prishli nemtsy: Ideinyi kollaboratsionizm v SSSR v period Velikoi Otechestvennoi voiny* (Moskva: ROSSPEN, 2012), 6. In this article, I nominally differentiate between the notions of "collaborator" and "collaborationist" in accordance with the principle that in the latter case the initiative to cooperate was not always met favorably.

ideological collaboration with the enemy; and non-ideological contacts with the occupation authorities. This literature has been deeply colored by the context in which it arose. In the post-war Soviet Union the notion of the "collaborationist," in John Austin's terminology, became "performative." Amir Weiner highlighted this process of "making sense" of the war experience in the title of his innovative work on the subject. As Weiner observes, even the mere fact of having refused to join a partisan unit and decided to stay on in occupied territory could later be viewed as acts constituting collaboration.[24]

When it comes to local collaborators in Ukraine, the situation only superficially appears to be clearcut. According to Ukrainian historians, among the police officers of Galicia, which is still considered the most anti-Soviet region of Ukraine, only a third were convinced enemies of the Soviet regime, while 40 percent of the officers acted under the pressure of particular circumstances.[25] A similar situation can be observed in the territory of the "Reichskomissariat Ukraine."[26] Among 33 people who became the members of the Ukrainian Cossack hundred organized in Zolotonosha in early December 1941, for example, only seven could be considered ideological enemies of the Bolsheviks, namely: two participants of the "Ukrainian revolution" of 1917–22; and five dispossessed kulaks/repressed people (that is, only 20 percent of the total number of the volunteers).[27]

The inhabitants' desire to collaborate within the guard-police structures had its downside for the German authorities. In the context of the general tendency of Nazi demographic policy on the occupied territory, collaborationism was a means of acquiring material goods.[28] As Günther Friedrich has vividly put it, work in a German

---

[24] Amir Weiner, *Making Sense of War: The Second World War and the Fate of the Bolshevik Revolution* (Princeton, NJ: Princeton University Press, 2001), 184–85.
[25] Oleg Klymenko, Serhii Tkachov, *Ukraintsi v politsii v dystrykti "Halychyna" (Chortkivs'kyi okrug): nimets'kii okupatsiinii rezhym v pivdennykh raionakh Ternopil'shhyny u 1941–1944 rr.* (Kharkiv: Ranok-NT, 2012), 274.
[26] Dereiko, *Mistsevi formuvannia*, 84.
[27] Ibid., 44.
[28] Ibid., 43.

canteen meant access to leftover food.[29] In this connection, a question arises whether coerced everyday contacts with the occupants that pursued the goal of mere survival should be classified as collaborationism. On the other hand, those who had decided to collaborate with the Germans did what they could to extract the maximum benefit from this. Officers of the Ukrainian auxiliary police forces[30]—the notorious *"politsai"* from Soviet cinema—used to steal from the production sites under their guard, later exchanging these stolen goods in barter. They also falsified bills for receiving deficit goods, and extorted ransom from Jews.[31] Some hired policemen finally had to be dismissed due to brawling, alcoholism, and thefts.[32]

In another case, soldiers of the local self-defense could act exclusively in the interests of their region without complying with orders from Rovno, the capital of the Reichskomissariat.[33] The phenomenon of the Polissian Sich—a large militia unit under the rule of field commander Taras Bul'ba -Borovets'—is a case in point.[34] This unit was initially called the "Ukrainian Insurgent Army," and was later merged into the armed units of the OUN-B. Initially, Bul'ba refused to subordinate to the Germans, stressing that he was a militia commander of Ukrainian units that considered the Ukrainian National Republic (UNR) rule legitimate in exile. It is not quite clear how such self-willed local "collaborationists" could have been of any real use to the German authorities.

---

[29] Friedrich, *Kollaboration in der Ukraine*, 187.
[30] In different parts of occupied Ukraine, these units formed from the locals were named differently ("police," "militia," "self-defense"). In this article, these terms are used interchangeably.
[31] Volodymyr Ginda and Ivan Dereiko, "Koruptsiia v raikhskomisariati 'Ukraiina': malovivchena storinka okupaciinoi diisnosti," in *Storinky voennoi istorii Ukrainy*, ed. Oleksander Lysenko (Kyiv: Instytut istorii Ukraiiny, 2011), vol. 14, 183.
[32] Iurii Oliinyk and Oleksander Zaval'niuk, *Natsists'kii okupatsiinyi rezhym v general'nii okruzi "Volyn'-Podillia" (1941–1944 rr.)* (Khmel'nits'kyi: Poligrafist-2, 2012), 61–62.
[33] Ivan Dereiko, "Lokal'nyi vymir partyzans'ko-politsiinogo protystoiannia v Raikhskomisariati 'Ukraiina': evoliutsiia sils'kykh viddilkiv politsii u 1941–1944 rr.," in *Storinky voennoii istorii Ukrainy*, ed. Oleksander Lysenko (Kyiv: Instytut istorii Ukraiiny, 2012), vol. 15, 87, 95.
[34] RGVA, f. 500k, op. 1, d. 775, l. 75.

Any attempt to integrate the OUN's activity into a complete picture of collaborationism on the occupied territory of Ukraine stumbles upon several serious obstacles. The first of these are issues of a purely legal nature. Those representatives of the OUN that were present in Galicia and Bukovina in autumn 1939, directly after the Red Army's "Liberation campaign," automatically became Soviet citizens. From this point of view, their collaborationism should be analyzed in a close relation with similar phenomena in other regions of Soviet Ukraine. At the same time, less than two years passed from the moment of the Soviet annexation of the Western Ukrainian regions until the German invasion, which raises the question of whether the local residents had enough time to become "Soviet people." This storyline becomes contradictory when we consider the fact that within the OUN, new Soviet citizens interacted and ideologically identified with emigrants who had never been citizens of the USSR.

Second, the OUN collaboration with the Nazis was initially ideological in nature, that is, the material component was either of secondary meaning or of no importance at all. By contrast, active collaborationists among the Soviet citizens who recognized the supremacy of the "New Order" were trying to maintain and where possible improve their status in the new circumstances. Compared to the realities of the occupation for ordinary people, officers of the militia were able to eke out a tolerable existence. For instance, in July 1942 Zaporozhian police officers received on a weekly basis 3.5 kilos of bread, and 10.5 kilos of potatoes and other products.[35] They also received monetary support: a daily allowance for commanders of subdivisions of the militia amounted to 1 Reichsmark, for common fighters—50 Reichspfennig.[36] In contrast, a young well-qualified worker in the occupied territory earned about 1.5 Reichsmark for an 11-hour working day.[37] Ironically, militia officers might sometimes be paid not only with German but also with Soviet money

---

[35] Frank Golczewski, "Die Kollaboration in der Ukraine" in *Kooperation und Verbrechen: Formen der "Kollaboration" im östlichen Europa, 1939–1945*, eds. Babette Quinkert, Tatjana Tönsmeyer (Göttingen: Wallstein, 2003), 174.
[36] RGVA, f. 1323k, op. 2, d. 276, l. 4 ob, 25.
[37] GARF, f. R7021, op. 148, d. 33, l. 17.

bearing the image of Lenin.³⁸ Ukrainian militia officers had an official right to social benefits, including medical treatment in local sanitoria in the event of being wounded on duty. Their families had the right to a pension in the event of the death of a breadwinner. Depending on their marital and parental status, age, rank, and some other factors, this pension amounted to 17 to 80 Reichsmark a month. There were also additional benefits for widows and orphans.³⁹

For their part, the OUN activists considered themselves the forerunners of the legitimate authorities of a future Ukraine. This was especially true for the "Banderites:" according to the instruction issued by their leader, the formation of Ukrainian statehood ought to commence on the Ukrainian territories liberated from "Muscovite-Bolshevik occupation" immediately, without any hesitation.⁴⁰ Following in the wake of the advancing German troops, the OUN members were trying to self-legalize within the institutions of the occupation authorities.⁴¹ As Ukrainian historians have shown, in more than 200 districts of Western and Central Ukraine lower rank bodies of the OUN had been formed and were awaiting the moment for legalization.⁴² The facts suggest that the nationalists probably wanted to use manifestations of collaborationism among the locals in order to pursue their own goals. As Yuri Radchenko puts it, the Ukrainian police force was a "school" for the OUN members in how to organizate mass ethnic cleansings.⁴³ Nationalists also seized upon the lack of discipline among Ukrainian policemen: on one occasion,

---

38   Nikolai Medved', *Okkupatsiia* (Moskva: Radio i sviaz', 1995), 28.
39   RGVA, f. 1323k, op. 2, d. 287, l. 2 ob, 5; Oliinyk and Zaval'niuk, *Natsists'kii okupatsiinii rezhym*, 56; and Dereiko, *Mistsevi formuvannia*, 87.
40   *Ukrainskie natsionalisticheskie organizatsii*. vol. 1, 299.
41   Dmitrii Titarenko, "Deiatel'nost' Organizatsii ukrainskikh natsionalistov v period natsistskoi okkupatsii na Vostoke Ukrainy (zona voennoi administratsii): kollaboratsiia ili soprotivlenie?" in *Problemy istorii massovykh politicheskikh repressii v SSSR: rol' SSSR vo Vtoroi mirovoi voine—neizvestnye i maloizuchennye stranitsy*, ed. Sergei Kropachev (Krasnodar: Volonter, 2006), 161.
42   Oliinyk and Zaval'niuk, *Natsists'kii okupatsiinii rezhym*, 44–46.
43   Yuri Radchenko, "'Ukrainische Hilfspolizei' i Holokost na territorii general-betsirka Chernigov, 1941–1943 gg.," *Forum noveishei vostochnoevropeiskoi istorii i kul'tury* 10, no. 1 (2013): 299.

for example, OUN agents purchased two machine guns from officers of the Vasilkov district police.[44]

All this may imply that Ukrainian nationalists (first and foremost, members of the OUN-B) considered themselves to be allies of Nazi Germany, rather than collaborators and subordinates. At the same time, from a political and legal point of view, Ukrainian nationalists lacked the attributes that would have allowed really putting them in line with the Reich's satellite countries, namely: statehood and a regular army. Here we return to the issue of the status of the OUN and its fractions—a status which was never clearly defined by the Germans.

As far as one can judge, the German side presumed that the OUN-M would agree to a subordinate status, while OUN-B was a small group of terrorists which would be easy to handle. As it turned out, however, the "Mel'nykovites" back-pedaled, bombarding Berlin with memoranda and waiting for at least a verbal indication of support, while the "Banderovites" immediately started to implement their policy without hesitation. The awkwardness of the situation was revealed very soon. It is clear that while Berlin initially planned to use the OUN-B in a subordinate status, the "Banderites" saw themselves as German allies. Possibly, in different circumstances, the German side may have wanted to have the OUN-M as an ally as well, however, the "Mel'nykovites" could offer themselves only as dependent collaborators. This significantly complicated the interaction of the occupation authorities with two differently directed groups of Ukrainian nationalists.

## "Strange" Allies: A Case of Situational Cooperation

World War II created numerous legal collisions without any precedent in either European or international law. One such collision was the "Phoney War." In this situation on the Western front from September 1939 to April 1940 Germany and its enemies, Great Britain and France, though formally at war, did not engage in fighting. Six months prior, in spring 1939, the Protectorate of Bohemia and

---

[44] Ginda and Dereiko, "Koruptsiia v raikhskomisariati 'Ukraiina,'" 181.

Moravia, created from the former Czechoslovakia, emerged on the map. This marked the first time that the term "protectorate" was applied to European realia—previously it had been used only for colonial possessions. In a similar way, the relationship between the Nazis and Ukrainian nationalists in 1941–43 also requires the formulation of a new terminology. Their interaction in occupied Ukraine did not correspond to the traditional frameworks and categories of collaborationism. At the same time, neither can this relationship be called an alliance. In fact, as I shall argue here, this can be more accurately described as a matter of situational cooperation.

The cooperation did not turn out to be productive for either side. Quite quickly mutual distrust appeared between the Germans and the OUN-B. Nevertheless, the German side continued to be in touch with the "Banderites," while the activity of the OUN-M, which was much weaker, was forcibly brought to naught by Berlin. Between these events, which peaked at the turn of the summer 1942, and the Ukrainian nationalists' invasion of the Soviet territory, an entire year passed. During this year, numerous actors, including German governmental and military structures as well as groups of Ukrainian nationalists, were testing their relative power, at times organizing new blocs or attacking others.

According to Rossoliński-Liebe, in exchange "for its services, the OUN-B expected political recompense in the form of a Ukrainian state,"[45] while "a well-planned program of actions" within the framework of "the Ukrainian national revolution" was not eventually realized, simply because "the OUN-B was unable to convince the Nazi authorities to agree with them."[46] I would take issue with this claim. An examination of the actions undertaken by Bandera's supporters indicates that, from a political point of view, these actions were in fact motivated by a mix of idealism and groundless ambitions. It is important to note that Bandera was not aiming to convince anyone of anything. Regardless of German guarantees and their own opportunities, the OUN-B leaders were determined to found their own state. This follows both from Bandera's pre-war

---

[45] Rossoliński-Liebe, "'Ukrainian National Revolution,'" 91.
[46] Ibid., 113.

instruction and from the implicit intention of Ukrainian nationalists to become a full-fledged party to a conflict, something which in reality was impossible without statehood and armed forces. It is not out of the question that Ukrainian nationalists' intention was to become, despite the lack of any objective prerequisites for this, a "third force."[47]

The ideological affinities of the NSDAP and the OUN added to Bandera's confidence that his followers would be willing to consider him an equal ally of the Reich in the fight against the Bolsheviks. This immediately found reflection on a symbolic level as well: in the rhetoric of OUN-B propaganda Hitler and Bandera were presented as located on the same level,[48] despite the fact that, in reality, they were clearly not comparable. In this context, it is little wonder that the proclamation of the Ukrainian state on 30 June 1941 became the first political act of the radical wing of the OUN. Yaroslav Stets'ko, Bandera's deputy, became the prime minister of the government, which was formed on the same day.

According to the documents, the formation of the Ukrainian government was completely unexpected for the German authorities. For instance, Georg Grosskopf, a Foreign Office expert on Russia,[49] wrote to Minister Ribbentrop that this "arbitrary undertaking of Bandera's vain group" had come as a total surprise for the German administration.[50] Meanwhile, Stets'ko's government wasted no time in advancing to the second phase aimed at institutionalizing the partnership between the OUN-B and the Germans, and proceeded to begin formation of its own armed forces. As early as in late June 1941, the OUN began to put together a local militia.[51] As research conducted by Ukrainian historians has shown, at the beginning of

---

[47] Titarenko, "Deiatel'nost' Organizatsii ukrainskikh natsionalistov," 169.
[48] Hannes Heer, "Einübung in den Holocaust: Lemberg Juni/Juli 1941," *Zeitschrift für Geschichtswissenschaft* 49 (2001): 417.
[49] Born and raised in the Russian Baltic provinces, Grosskopf served as a German diplomat in Russia before the Revolution and then made a career in the German Foreign Ministry. His last position in the Soviet Union was Consul General in Kyiv (1937–38).
[50] *Akten zur deutschen auswärtigen Politik 1918–1945.* Serie D. Bd. XIII.1 (Göttingen: Vandenhoeck & Ruprecht, 1970), 167.
[51] *Ukrainskie natsionalisticheskie organizatsii,* vol. 1, 331.

the occupation the OUN-B managed to equip this militia fully with its own staff.⁵² Moreover, the commanders of "Bandera's" "March units" (*pokhidny grupy*) vouched to form national military garrisons in settlements for the future establishment of a Ukrainian people's revolutionary army.⁵³ According to Bandera's pre-war instruction, this army was supposed to draw upon, among other sources, the "Ukrainian units" of the Red Army.⁵⁴

As we have seen, the different participants of the events in the occupied territory were each trying to implement their own agenda. This brought to life a number of processes that could take place simultaneously, intersect, and continue or complement one another. What is of importance here is that each side may have given the same events a different meaning. In this connection, the case of L'viv, which was occupied by the Germans on 30 June 1941, is of special significance. The Ukrainian nationalists who accompanied the Germans into the city began a horrifying anti-Jewish pogrom that continued to rage for the entire following week. As Hannes Heer remarks, the Wehrmacht units and provost corps had no objection to using Ukrainian combatants to carry out this "dirty work" while they would just supervise it, for instance, when it came to incarcerating or separating Jews.⁵⁵ In this way, for the Germans, Ukrainian nationalists were willing volunteers.

The OUN members perceived this pogrom in a completely different way. In their view, the proclamation of statehood, establishment of an army, and Jew-baiting were all parts of one broader process, namely, the formation of "the Ukrainian nation," as they saw it. According to witnesses who survived the L'viv events, "people with yellow-blue bandages suddenly showed up and began to establish their own 'order.'"⁵⁶ Subsequently, as German troops advanced across Ukraine, armed units of the OUN rendered them help in

---

[52] Oliinyk and Zaval'niuk, *Natsists'kii okupatsiinii rezhym*, 57.
[53] Dereiko, "Lokal'nyi vymir," 89.
[54] *Ukrainskie natsionalisticheskie organizatsii*, vol. 1, 298.
[55] Heer, "Einübung in den Holocaust," 419.
[56] Ibid., 418.

fighting against the remaining Soviet assets in the occupied territory.⁵⁷

These two storylines are offered here as illustrative cases of what happened when the initial intentions of the Nazis and the OUN coincided. However, this was by no means always the case. The German military authorities which initially supported the self-organization of the Ukrainians who arrived together with the Wehrmacht units, changed their opinion after the events in L'viv. In early July 1941, it was decided to strengthen the military population in the interests of securing the front divisions' advancement and to organize command posts "in the conditions when thousands of Ukrainian nationalists were operating in L'viv."⁵⁸ A similar action was undertaken by the civilian administration that now demanded of the OUN-B leaders that they terminate the authority of the Ukrainian state bodies. After Bandera and Stets'ko sabotaged the decision of the German authorities on 5 July 1941, they were detained and placed under house arrest. During the following week, other members of the failed Ukrainian government were also arrested.

At the same time, the issue was that the OUN-B's area of activity was not limited to L'viv and Galicia. Armed units of Ukrainian nationalists were advancing almost simultaneously with the Wehrmacht. In August 1941, they were already in Volhynia, in September they were in Kyiv, and by November "March units" of the organization had reached the Donbas. There the Germans decided to use a two-sided approach—to try to use the OUN-M and neutralize the OUN-B's military units at the same time.

A curious detail, important for the current research on this topic, relates to these storylines. Decades later, in emigration, Pyotr Mirchuk, a close associate of Bandera and the most famous historiographer of the OUN, wrote that in fact Mel'nyk had been a mere executioner of Hitler's will. In Mirchuk's view, the OUN-M leader's actions were out of line with Bandera's noble intent to revive the Ukrainian state. In this context, Mirchuk accused Mel'nyk of the most serious crime: the intention to hand over Ukrainian territory

---

57   Titarenko, "Deiatel'nost' Organizatsii ukrainskikh natsionalistov," 162, 167.
58   Heer, "Einübung in den Holocaust," 422.

to German control. This intention helped to explain Mel'nyk's withdrawal from "the act of 30 June," while his "strong desire" to serve Germany was allegedly seen as "backstabbing" by Bandera.[59]

In the understanding of Bandera's fraction, then, unconditional adherence to the German line constituted collaborationism, as opposed to the "alliance" with the Germans which was viewed as an inevitable contingency of war. In Bandera's instruction, this alliance was called "natural." Such an alliance was permissible not only with the Reich but with any state waging the "Fight with the Muscovites," so long as they were not hostile to Ukraine.[60] From the point of view of the "Banderites," the situation in which "Mel'nykovites" found themselves was, by contrast, the position of a subordinate. Armed units organized by the OUN-M military activists—the Bukovina and Kyiv combat units *(kurens)*—continued to cooperate with the Germans even after they were merged and reformed into the local police. The units that, in their turn, were formed by the OUN-B were either let go or reformed into units subordinate to German punitive divisions or into working groups in August–October 1941.[61]

In this case, Bandera's anger, especially in the context of the failed L'viv government, was probably a response to the Mel'nyk fraction's political activity.[62] In October 1941, an OUN-M activist Volodymyr Bahaziy became burgomaster of Kyiv. At the same time, a Ukrainian National Council was established, with the aim of coordinating the organization of Ukrainian governing bodies. The newspaper *Ukrainian Word* provided informational support for the Council. In this sense, it was no coincidence that the assassinations of Mel'nyk's de facto representatives in occupied Ukraine, Mykola Stsibors'kyi and Omelian Senyk, were tied to the name of the OUN-B leader.

---

[59] Petro Mirchuk, *Revoliutsiinii zmag za USSD* (New York-Toronto: Soiuz ukrains'kykh politv'iazniv, 1985), vol. 1, 8–10, 36, 103.
[60] *Ukrainskie natsionalisticheskie organizatsii*, vol. 1, 299.
[61] Dereiko, "Lokal'nyi vymir," 94.
[62] Karel C. Berkhoff, *Harvest of Despair: Life and Death in Ukraine under Nazi Rule* (Cambridge, MA: Harvard University Press, 2004), 52.

The "Mel'nykovites'" enthusiasm and their ambitious plans could not have remained unnoticed by the German authorities. Stability in the rear was of special importance in the conditions of the Wehrmacht attack on Moscow in October–November 1941. During this time, the Ukrainian National Council was dissolved by order of the Reichskommissar of Ukraine, Erich Koch. In February 1942, burgomaster Bahaziy, editor of the *Ukrainian Word* Ivan Rogach, and other OUN-M activists were arrested and executed. Repressions against Mel'nyk's fraction continued for the entire year of 1942. Having deprived the militarized formations of the "Mel'nykovites" of their political leadership, the Nazis effectively turned them into ordinary collaborationists, similar to those who were representatives of the local communities.

It would appear that a similar fate had been planned for the "Banderites." The first arrests of the OUN-B's active members started as early as in early September 1941, and, what is more, not only within the territory of Ukraine.[63] In the western and central regions of Ukraine, the staff of the militia was fully changed with a view to eradicating the influence of Bandera's activists. In the East, the new militia staff got rid of non-loyal Ukrainian nationalists.[64] Electivity of commanders was abolished,[65] and combatants themselves started to submit only formally to a local burgomaster located, in fact, under Gestapo supervision.[66] The battalions *Nachtigall* and *Roland*, composed of Bandera's cadres, were re-deployed in October 1941 to Frankfurt/Oder. Relatively soon after that, the 201st battalion of Schutzmanschaft (security divisions) was organized.[67]

The Germans' massive attack disorganized and disoriented the OUN-B. At first, the "Banderites" met this drastic change in the attitude of their "allies" with disbelief: in early October 1941, it was

---

[63] Stanislav Kulchyts'kii (ed.), *Organizatsiia ukraiins'kykh natsionalistiv i Ukrains'ka povstans'ka armiia: istorychni narysy* (Kyïv: Naukova dumka, 2005), 91.
[64] Radchenko, "'Ukrainische Hilfspolizei' i Holokost," 304.
[65] Dereiko, "Lokal'nyi vymir," 95.
[66] Russian State Archive of Socio-Political History (RGASPI), f. 17, op. 125, d. 172, l. 13.
[67] Grzegorz Motyka, *Ot volynskoi rezni do operatsii "Visla". Pol'sko-ukrainskii konflikt 1943-1947* (Moscow: ROSSPEN, 2014), 41.

decided, in a political sense, not to enter into conflict with the Germans and not to conduct an openly anti-German propaganda line.[68] Nevertheless, the prospect of becoming waste material in the Nazis' hands was not just unattractive for "Banderites;" it also contradicted the whole political program of the OUN-B. In early 1942, OUN brochures in which Germany was named "an eternal enemy" appeared in Vinnitsa.[69] In April of the same year, at the OUN-B's 2nd Congress, Germany was formally acknowledged "an occupant" of Ukraine.[70] The German side retaliated in kind: by May 1942 all OUN-B activists who did not agree with the Reich's line were labeled in the official documents as representatives of "an illegal movement."[71] Ukrainian symbolism was also attacked. Earlier established local armed divisions were dissolved for adjuration to Ukraine under a yellow-blue flag,[72] and by the end of 1942, Ukrainian symbols had disappeared from the entire territory of the Reichskomissariat.[73]

By that time, "Bandera's" fraction of the OUN found itself in a rather complicated situation. Bandera and Stets'ko were under arrest, and political activists were being persecuted and killed by the Germans. *Nachtigall* and *Roland's* combatants were in Belarus until the very end of 1942, and turned into collaborationists, taking part in punitive and anti-partisan actions. The OUN-B had been torn apart by the internal contradictions over which position to take towards the Reich. An answer to this question would soon be delivered, however, by the ensuing events on the Soviet–German front.

**Accomplices to War Crimes or Resistance Fighters?**

German army advances during the summer campaign of 1942 in the East, in contradiction to the Wehrmacht General Staff plans, did not bring the crucial victory. The protracted Battle of Stalingrad ended

---

[68] Kulchyts'kii (ed.), *Organizatsiia ukrains'kykh natsionalistiv i Ukraiins'ka povstans'ka armiia: istorichni narysy*, 92.
[69] Weiner, *Making Sense of War*, 165.
[70] Titarenko, "Deiatel'nost' Organizatsii ukrainskikh natsionalistov," 167.
[71] RGVA, f. 500k, op. 1, d. 775, l. 71.
[72] Dereiko, "Lokal'nyi vymir," 90–91.
[73] Berkhoff, *Harvest of Despair*, 53.

in a crushing defeat for the Germans in February 1943. The Red Army's strategic advantage was established because of successful battles near Kursk in July 1943. Only a month later, after Kharkov was seized, Soviet army was ready to start the attack on Ukraine along a broad front.

Before the summer fighting, the OUN political leadership operated under the illusion that the defeat of Germany was imminent. Within this illusion, the role of Ukraine's chief enemy was reserved for the USSR or Poland, or both. In this connection, a member of the OUN's General Council Mykhailo Stepaniak, who claimed leadership in the organization, offered to stir up a revolt against Germany with a view to enabling the invasion of Ukraine before the Red Army's appearance. This was supposed to deepen the conflict between the Western allies and the Soviet Union, possibly even bringing them to war with one another.[74] The grounds of this restoration of the relationship with the Germans were not only military. The realities of the two years of Nazi occupation and the influx into the OUN of representatives of the new generation, including former citizens of Soviet Ukraine, led to a shift in the organization's worldview,[75] which had to be adjusted to the new conditions.

Stepaniak's proposal was supported by Mykola Lebed', the OUN-B's acting leader (who stood in for Bandera after he was arrested), but it clashed with the position of Roman Shukhevych, a recognized leader of the military wing of the organization. In Shukhevych's view, independent Ukraine's main enemy was the Soviet Union, and conflict with the Germans was a matter of inevitable "self-defense." At the 3rd Extraordinary Congress of the OUN-B in August 1943 a merger of certain elements of both platforms took place. On the one hand, the ethnic approach to "the Ukrainian nation" in theory was formally renounced, and the post-partisan nature of the OUN was declared. At the same time, the concept of a "fight with two imperialisms" (that is, German and Russian) was voiced. In spring 1943, under Shukhevych and Dmytro Kliachkivs'kyi, guerrilla troops began to be formed into the UPA. Rather

---

[74] Motyka, *Ot volynskoi rezni do operatsii "Visla,"* 62.
[75] Primachenko, "Evoliutsiia natsional'nogo voprosa," 396–97.

quickly, its fighters managed to suppress their "competitors"—the OUN-M troops and "Bul'bovites."

It should be noted that in the context of the substantial German defeats taking place at the time, these declarations were made in order to secure the OUN's position vis-à-vis the Allies. In reality, as we know, there was no real intention to implement them (as the subsequent actions of the Ukrainian nationalists showed). The first two provisions were obviously formalities rather than functioning regulations. As the Ukrainian historian Ihor Il'iushin has put it, there is enough evidence from the documents to create a general picture of anti-Polish actions carried out by the OUN-UPA in Volhynia.[76] The Ukrainian nationalists' contribution to the Holocaust has also been documented in the literature.[77] A political component was still of great importance: "Banderites" did not consider Borovets their ally, even though he also looked upon the "rabid Gestapo" and "Moscow oprichniks" as enemies.[78] As for the third provision, as Anatoliy Kentiy points out, initially the UPA actions were rather aimed at "self-defense of the Ukrainian population" in the occupied territory, and the UPA did not strive to pick an open fight with the Germans with their superior forces. Railroads, military commandants' headquarters and concentrations of munitions were "beyond the scope" of the insurgents.[79] As Grzegorz Motyka puts it, for obvious reasons the OUN-B was not interested in weakening the Wehrmacht that was fighting against the USSR.[80]

Therefore, we may see a variety of activities carried out by Ukrainian nationalists (primarily, Bandera's fraction of the OUN) in the first two years of the "War in the East." We witnessed examples of specific quasi-ally relations between Ukrainian nationalists and the Nazis in the first two summer months (late June–late August) of

---

[76] Ihor Il'iushyn, *Volins'ka tragediia 1943–1944 rr.* (Kyiv: Instytut istorii Ukraiiny, 2003), 196.
[77] Q.v. works by John-Paul Himka, Per Rudling and the latest book by Kai Struve, *Deutsche Herrschaft, ukrainischer Nationalismus, antijüdische Gewalt: Der Sommer 1941 in der Westukraine* (Berlin: De Gryuter, 2015).
[78] RGASPI, f. 69, op. 1, d. 578, l. 17 ob.
[79] *Organizatsiia ukraiins'kikh natsionalistiv i Ukraiins'ka povstans'ka armiia: istorichni narysi*, 183–84.
[80] Motyka, *Ot volynskoi rezni do operatsii "Visla,"* 64.

1941. On the other hand, a lengthier period of collaborationism (the year-long service of "Banderites" in the 201st battalion of the Schutzmannschaft from December 1941 to December 1942) cannot be denied. The split in the OUN significantly affects categorization of the actions of Ukrainian nationalists. When the actions of a division are under consideration, it should be specified which fraction and period one has in mind. This significantly complicates the creation of a unified picture of the organization's activities.

The hardest task appears to be untangling the references to the two sides that collaborated with the Nazis—the OUN, on the one hand, and Soviet collaborationists among the locals, on the other. Endless variants and combinations were possible. For instance, the OUN-B emissaries could ideologically mobilize the militia in a certain district. In such a case, the militia's participation in punitive operations against Jews could be interpreted both as collaborationism with the Germans and as a part of the OUN strategy to establish "the Ukrainian nation." On the other hand, there were cases of apolitical policemen (who comprised, as studies have shown, 70–80 percent of the total[81]) who considered themselves to be German personnel, but whose services were "turned down" by the German administration, who moved to dissolve their units in a reaction to the OUN's willfulness.

As Günter Friedrich states, the relationship between the Germans and collaborationists—both "ideological" and "forced" ones—were of a mutually pragmatic nature.[82] This corresponds with Grzegorz Rossoliński-Liebe's remark that the unsuccessful attempt by the OUN-B to gain support from the Nazis for its own state project did not mean that the "Banderites" fought against the latter during the "Ukrainian national revolution".[83] Nevertheless, this pragmatic approach quickly revealed its downside. The relationship between the initial contractors—the Nazis and the Ukrainian nationalists—de facto came down to a matter of situational cooperation. Collaborationists among Soviet citizens mostly were trying to strengthen

---

[81] Dereiko, *Mistsevi formuvannia*, 44.
[82] Friedrich, *Kollaboration in der Ukraine*, 71.
[83] Rossoliński-Liebe, "'Ukrainian National Revolution,'" 90.

and maintain their status in the given situation, rather than to participate in the realization of the Nazis' program as such. The occupying authorities realized rather quickly that they could not rely on either of these groups. In this sense, it can be said that all the parties to the process miscalculated in their own way.

\* \* \*

This article has set out less to provide answers than to pose questions. Given the complexity of the topic, this should be unsurprising. From the scholarly point of view, providing an exact classification of the Nazis' cooperation with Ukrainian nationalists and collaborationists among the locals in occupied Ukraine is extremely problematic. This is in part because the processes under study refuse to fit into the convenient and comprehensible categories. Instead, they intertwine, flow out of another, and go their separate ways, only to converge yet again.

It is possible that precisely this difficulty may have been a factor pushing Soviet historiography into lumping all Ukrainian collaborationists together into a single entity of "traitors." At the same time, as Amir Weiner has brought into sharp focus, in fact Soviet investigative bodies considered each case from the viewpoint of possible "abetting of occupants."[84] Those who belonged to the OUN and the Ukrainian Insurgent Army *(Ukraiins'ka Povstans'ka Armiia, UPA)* were always singled out and placed in a special category—"Ukrainian bourgeois nationalists"—and were a priori seen as instruments of the "Hitlerites."

The research on the occupation period carried out by Ukrainian historians after the collapse of the USSR stumbled when it came to the question of how to categorize Ukrainian nationalists' actions, partly because, as we have seen, not all of these can be interpreted as collaborationism. In 1997, by a special decree of Ukrainian President Leonid Kuchma, a governmental commission was organized with the aim of conducting research on OUN-UPA activities during World War II. The commission's work has in turn also become the

---

[84] Weiner, *Making Sense of War*, 83f.

subject of debate, especially insofar as it touched upon the storylines of the UPA's cooperation with the Germans and the casualties it suffered when fighting against them. On the other hand, the nation-building process in post-Soviet Ukraine has returned to the society the narrative which was preserved in the diaspora tradition, whereby the Ukrainians are viewed as caught "between two imperialisms/totalitarianisms." This narrative's value for nationalists lies in the fact that it has allowed, and continues to allow today, the blurring out of all contradiction. This is not only a consequence of the complexity involved in distinguishing "allies," "collaborators," and "collaborationists" when it comes to the history of occupied Ukraine. The contemporary ultra-nationalist motto "nation above all" and the labeling of the UPA as as a "Resistance movement" (*Rukh oporu*) against occupying forces whose ideas in fact did not differ greatly from those expressed by these mottoes is also an important dimension to this.

Why did the narrative of radical nationalism embodied in the person of Stepan Bandera gain its popularity, at least on the emotional level? As far as we can assume, two crucial points condition his authority among Ukrainian right-wing radicals, as noted by Rossoliński-Liebe in his reference to Bandera's "afterlife" in the subtitle of his work. First, he represents an image of a passionate Hero, typical for "romantic nationalism." Bandera's life and death have become an embodiment of the motto "nation above all." Historical events are substituted by a mythologized narrative, which is invoked by reference groups in order to shape their identity.

No less important is the fact that Bandera's radicalism has become a kind of reaction to the defeat in the "War for Independence" in 1917–21, a response to the weakness of Ukrainian national democrats.[85] The romantic view on the activities of the Ukrainian nationalists during World War II damaged the image of Mykhailo Hrushevsky, the first leader of independent Ukraine, who was regarded as a national hero back in the early 1990s. In this conception Hrushevsky, despite holding real power and avowed authority, not only surrendered and withdrew from politics, but also returned to

---

[85] Primachenko, "Evoliutsiia natsional'nogo voprosa," 398.

Russia, while Bandera, who actually possessed dubious power and glory as a statesman, continued to fight for Ukraine until his last breath. Nationalists' attraction to the charismatic leader Bandera (and not to the cabinet intellectual Hrushevsky) is quite explicable in this case.[86]

Though the figure of Konovalets' is also used nowadays in the symbolic space by Ukrainian nationalists, its prevalence is incomparable with that of Bandera. The same is true of Mel'nyk, the closest companion of Konovalets', but the bitter rival of the "Banderites". Both of Bandera's older comrades were displaced by another passionate "Man of Action"—chief of the UPA, Roman Shukhevych. This duumvirate has come to embody the OUN–UPA connection, both in the rhetoric of Ukrainian nationalists and in the view of their enemies as well. It is remarkable that neither Konovalets' nor Mel'nyk, in their turn, received any formal recognition of their activity in post-Soviet Ukraine, such as conferment of the title of Hero.

It is worth mentioning that, unlike national democrats who offered the conception of a Ukrainian state,[87] nationalists had only a vague image of the process of formation of future Ukraine. In their view, the first stage was supposed to be "liberation struggle" and subsequent establishment of the national dictatorship.[88] It was not initially clarified in which form both phenomena should be realized, however, according to Bandera, the only way to liberation was "national revolution."[89] This ideological cliché meant unification of all Ukrainians under the auspices of the OUN in the fight for their sovereignty. It is this concept of "national revolution" that became, as Rossoliński-Liebe puts it, "the missing link" between the Ukrainian state proclaimed in 1941 and the OUN-B's participation in anti-

---

[86] A parallel might be drawn here to the case of Kosovo, where it is the figure of Adem Jashari, a brutal field commander, who serves as national hero for the Kosovan Albanians, and not the founder of the Kosovan statehood, Professor Ibrahim Rugova.

[87] Aleksandr Dergachev (ed.), *Ukrainskaia gosudarstvennost' v XX veke: Istoriko-politologicheskii analiz* (Kyiv: Politychna dumka, 1996), 18–22.

[88] Heorhii Kas'ianov, *Do pytannia pro ideolohiiu Orhanizatsii ukraiins'kikh natsionalistiv (OUN): Analitichnyi ohliad* (Kyiv: Instytut istorii Ukraiiny, 2003), 15–16.

[89] Stepan Bandera, *Perspektivy ukrains'koi revoliutsii* (Drogobych: Vidrodzhennia, 1998), 267.

Jewish pogroms and collaboration with the Nazis.[90] Such attention towards Bandera and Shukhevych indicates that the events of World War II and attempts to establish sovereignty directly in the territory of Ukraine are of foremost importance for nationalists today.

Here we return to the topos of "Heroes who Fought for Ukraine"—a topos which refers exclusively to the OUN-B, since only the "Banderites" were fighting for the true interest of the "Ukrainian nation" and only they can, therefore, represent *Rukh oporu*. As we can see, the actions of the OUN-M and other political forces do not find any reflection here—for various reasons, they were stigmatized, either as "opportunists" who abetted the Germans (sic!) or as ideologically alien to the principle of the "Ukrainian nation." This is why the title of Hero of Ukraine was bestowed upon Bandera and Shukhevych, but not on the "traitor" Mel'nyk, and not even on Konovalets' with his "preparatory work." A no less important storyline relates to the fact that, ultimately, the idea of the struggle against the "enemies of Ukraine" is aimed at legitimizing all the actions of the OUN-B and the UPA, both during and after the Nazi occupation. In light of this, the issue of whether the Ukrainian nationalists should be categorized as the Nazis' allies or collaborationists is relegated to the background, while the issue of researching their own crimes on the occupied territory moves to center-stage.

---

[90] Rossoliński-Liebe, "'Ukrainian National Revolution,'" 84.

# Volodymyr Viatrovych's
## *Second Polish-Ukrainian War*[*]

Myroslav Shkandrij

**Abstract:** *The article reviews Volodymyr Viatrovych's book* Druha pols'ko-ukrains'ka viina, 1942-1947 *(The Second Polish-Ukrainian War, 1942-1947), which was published in Kyiv in 2012 and immediately sparked an international debate. The focus is on Viatrovych's view of events in Volhynia in 1943, his representation of the OUN's role in these events, and the wider issue of cultural memory politics in contemporary Ukraine. It argues that Viatrovych successfully challenges some settled opinions among both Polish and Western scholars but undermines his case by unproblematically treating the OUN as a liberation movement and by avoiding a number of key issues.*

Volodymyr Viatrovych's controversial book, *The Second Polish–Ukrainian War, 1942–1947*, was published in Ukraine in 2012.[1] The book immediately sparked an international debate, forming the topic, for example, of a special issue of the international journal *Ab Imperio: Studies of New Imperial History and Nationalism in the Post-Soviet Space*.[2] In 2016, Viatrovych published substantially the same book and argument under a different title, *Behind the Scenes of "Volyn 43": The Unknown Polish-Ukrainian War*.[3] By that time the

---

[*] This paper is based on a presentation delivered at the 12th Annual Danyliw Seminar, Chair of Ukrainian Studies, University of Ottawa, on 10–12 November 2016.
[1] Volodymyr Viatrovych, *Druha pols'ko-ukrains'ka viina, 1942-1947*, 2nd revised ed. (Kyiv: Vydavnychyi dim "Kyievo-Mohylians'ka Akademiia, 2012).
[2] Sofia Grachova, Ihor Il'iushyn, Grzegorz Motyka, Per Anders Rudling, and Andrzej Zięba contributed to the discussion. See "Forum. Volodymyr Viatrovych. Druha pols'ko-ukrains'ka viina 1942-1947. Kyiv: Vydavnychyi dim Kyievo-Mohylians'ka Akademiia, 2011," *Ab imperio* no. 1 (2012): 351–433.
[3] Volodymyr Viatrovych, *Za lashtunkamy "Volyni-43": Nevidoma pols'ko-ukrains'ka viina* (Kharkiv: Knyhoklub, 2016).

issue of how to characterize the Polish–Ukrainian conflict in the 1940s had begun to resonate widely as politicians and the public in both Ukraine and Poland became involved. On 22 July 2016 the Polish parliament recognized the events in Volhynia as a genocide, when it passed a resolution "in memory of the victims of genocide ... committed by Ukrainian nationalists from 1943–1945, who murdered over 100,000 inhabitants of the Second Polish Republic."[4] In response, on 25 August ninety prominent Ukrainian intellectuals and politicians called upon the Ukrainian parliament to establish three remembrance days for Ukrainian victims of crimes committed by Poles.[5] Shortly afterwards *Wołyń*, a Polish feature film dramatizing the massacres of 1943, was released.[6] In both scholarly discourse and memory politics played out in mass media, Viatrovych's book has played a prominent role, particularly concerning the Volhynian events of 1943–44.[7] The Polish government's sharp turn to the right

---

[4] "Sejm przyjal uchwale w sprawie wolynia ze stwierdzeniem o ludobójstwie," *Wyborcza.pl*, 22 July 2016, http://wyborcza.pl/1,75398,20436098,sejm-przyjal-uchwale-w-sprawie-wolynia-ze-stwierdzeniem-o-ludobojstwie.html?disableRedirects=true (accessed 6 April 2018).

[5] Mikhail Klikushin, "From Friends to Bitter Rivals: Poland and Ukraine Accuse Each Other of 'Genocide'," *observer.com*, 1 September 2016, http://observer.com/2016/09/from-friends-to-bitter-rivals-poland-and-ukraine-accuse-each-other-of-genocide (accessed 6 April 2018).

[6] For a review see Simon Lewis, "Wolyn: Towards a Memory Dialogue between Poland and Ukraine," *Open Democracy*, 27 October 2016, https://www.opendemocracy.net/od-russia/simon-lewis/wolyn-towards-memory-dialogue-poland-ukraine (accessed 6 April 2018). For a Ukrainian reaction to the politicization of issues in this film see Iurii Vynnychuk, "Pliundrovani Kresy," *Zbruc*, 23 October 2016, http://zbruc.eu/node/57747 (accessed 6 April 2018).

[7] For examples see Josh Cohen, "The Historian Whitewashing Ukraine's Past," *Foreign Policy*, 2 May 2016, https://foreignpolicy.com/2016/05/02/the-historian-whitewashing-ukraines-past-volodymyr-viatrovych; Halyna Coynash, "Politicizing History: Parliament Adopts Dangerously Divisive Laws," *Human Rights in Ukraine*, 10 April 2016, http://khpg.org/en/index.php?id=1428632777_(accessed 6 April 2018) and "Kremlin-faked Polish-Ukrainian Relations, *Human Rights in Ukraine*, 2 November 2016, http://khpg.org/en/index.php?id=1446155700 (accessed 6 April 2018); Alexander J. Motyl, "Trivializing Genocide: A Dangerous Distraction, *World Affairs*, 18 August 2016, http://www.worldaffairsjournal.org/blog/alexander-j-motyl/trivializing-genocide-dangerous-distraction (accessed 6 April 2018); Mariya Shchur, "Are Scholars from the Institute of National Memory 'Whitewashing' the History of Ukraine? Volodymyr Viatrovych Responds to Josh Cohen's Article in Foreign Policy," *Euromaidan Press*, 4 May

after the election of the Law and Justice party in 2015, efforts by the Russian government to undermine Polish–Ukrainian relations by using memory conflicts after the Euromaidan Revolution of 2013–14, and the general regional trend toward the political mobilization of history have all given prominence to the Volhynian issue, making Viatrovych a whipping boy in some circles, while simultaneously boosting his reputation in others. This paper offers an analysis of his 2012 book in the light of critical commentary.

\*\*\*

Viatrovych first became a household name in Ukraine in 2002 when he was appointed the first director of the Center for Research into the Liberation Movement *(Tsentr Doslidzhen Vyzvolnoho Rukhu,* TsDVR) and began vigorously promoting a heroic narrative of the OUN(b) (Organization of Ukrainian Nationalists (Bandera faction) and UPA (Ukrainian Insurgent Army) in the media. He held the post until 2008 when President Viktor Yushchenko made him head of the State Archives of the Security Service of Ukraine (HDA SBU). During Yushchenko's term in office the heroic narrative became more prominent as streets were renamed in honor of OUN and UPA leaders, and Stepan Bandera was designated a "Hero of Ukraine." Viatrovych lent his support to this campaign and was frequently quoted in the media. In an article from 2010, for example, he argued:

> The struggle of Ukrainians for independence is one of the cornerstones of our national self-identification. Therefore without the UPA, without Bandera, without [Roman] Shukhevych there would not be a contemporary Ukrainian state, there would not be a contemporary Ukrainian nation. The fundamental values of the Ukrainian movement, expressed in the manifesto of the OUN under the leadership of Stepan Bandera in December 1940 in the

---

2016, http://euromaidanpress.com/2016/05/04/92324 (accessed 6 April 2018); Vitalii Portnikov, "Poland and Politics: Why Politicians Should Not Meddle in History," *Euromaidan Press*, 3 September 2016, http://euromaidanpress.com/2016/09/03/poland-and-political-gains-why-politicians-should-not-meddle-in-history/#arvlbdata (accessed 6 April 2016); and Serhii Riabenko, "'Druzhe Ruban!' Vykorystannia falsyfikativ v dyskusiikh pro Volyn," *Istorychna Pravda*, 23 October 2016, http://www.istpravda.com.ua/articles/2016/10/22/149259 (accessed 6 April 2016).

slogan "Freedom for nations! Freedom for the individual!" are values on which the contemporary united Europe rests.[8]

After Yushchenko lost the presidency in 2010, Viatrovych spent a short time as a research fellow at the Harvard Ukrainian Research Institute. He continued publishing articles on Ukrainian history, and shortly after the Euromaidan Revolution, in March 2014, he was appointed Director of the Ukrainian Institute of National Memory (UINP, sometimes translated as Institute of National Remembrance).

His most controversial and important text is *Druha pols'ko-ukrains'ka viina, 1942-1947*, the second, revised, and expanded edition of which appeared in 2012. A Polish translation was published in 2013 and an English translation is planned.[9] The book's first edition came out in conjunction with a two-volume collection of documents edited by Viatrovych and entitled *Pols'ko-ukrains'ki stosunky v 1942-1947 rokakh u dokumentakh OUN ta UPA* (Polish-Ukrainian Relations in 1942-1947 in Documents of the OUN and UPA, 2011). In preparing the book and compiling the documents, he was able to use materials in the HDA SBU (Security Service of Ukraine) archive, which he headed in the years 2008-10. He also made use of the Mykola Lebed papers at the Harvard Ukrainian Research Institute, and materials at the archive of the Center for Research into the Liberation Movement (TsDVR) in L'viv (located in the Museum of the Lontskyi Prison), the Central State Archive of Civic Organizations (TsDAHO), and other major archival collections in Kyiv. The second revised edition added materials from the Volodymyr Kubijovic archive in the Library and Archives of Canada, Ottawa, which contain substantial documentation on events in the Chełm region (Kholm in Ukrainian). For this edition Viatrovych also added information from the files in Ukraine's archives that record the interrogations of

---

[8] Volodymyr Viatrovych, "Ievropa zahovoryla," *Ukrains'ka Pravda*, 2 March 2010, http://www.pravda.com.ua/columns/2010/03/2/4824766 (accessed 6 April 2018).

[9] For the Polish translation see Wołodymyr Wiatrowycz, *Druga Wojna Polsko-Ukraińska, 1942-1947* (Warsaw: Archiwum Ukraińskie, 2013).

UPA fighters, interrogations that were conducted by Soviet forces after the war.

Viatrovych's book succeeds in mounting a convincing challenge to what he views as tendentious anti-Ukrainian Polish commentary on this history. For example, he exposes the Polish media's incorrect attribution of photographs and the heavily biased way in which the discussion of Volhynia has been conducted in Poland since 2003.[10] He objects to use of the term genocide in connection with events in Volhynia in 1943–44, arguing instead that the Polish-Ukrainian conflict should be situated within the wider framework of a long-standing war that dates back at least to 1918–19. As for the violence in Volhynia itself, he maintains that "the first armed clashes in the Chełm/Kholm region in the summer of 1942 can be considered the beginning of the war, and its final act was the Vistula Operation (Akcja Wisła), which ended in July 1947."[11] The book also gives prominence to the armed struggle in the Zakerzonnia (the territories beyond the Curzon line: Chełm, Podlachie, Nadsianie and the Lemko region) in 1945–47, and to the expulsion of the Ukrainian population from these lands immediately after the war. The revised edition contains an entire new section devoted to this issue.[12] The author demonstrates how both the Polish government-in-exile and the Ukrainian underground failed to come to an agreement because of their conflicting claims to the territories of Volhynia, Galicia, and Zakerzonnia. To a degree Viatrovych succeeds in complicating the picture of the war. The tangled skein of conflicts in this part of the world has been remarked upon by scholars. This is how Yaroslav Hrytsak, whom Viatrovych quotes, describes the situation:

> When dealing with events in Volhynia in the spring of 1943 we have to account for several factors: the "macrowar" between the Nazis and the Soviet state, two superpowers; the "microwar" between Polish, Ukrainian and Soviet undergrounds; a small civil war between various groups in the Ukrainian underground (such as the conflict between the banderites, the bulbashites

---

[10] Volodymyr Viatrovych, *Druha pols'ko-ukrains'ka viina, 1942–1947*, 2nd revised ed. (Kyiv: Vydavnychyi dim "Kyievo-Mohylians'ka akademiia," 2012), 24 and 307–23. (Original edition Kyievo-Mohylians'ka Akademiia, 2011.)
[11] Ibid., 39.
[12] Ibid., 243–303.

and the melnykites, or the competition for power within the newly-created UPA between Galician and Volhynian groups); a peasant war for the land; and, finally, the simple criminal dregs *[bandytske shumovynnia]*, which exploited the war and were widespread in the Volhynian forests. To complete the picture, we could add the destruction of Volhynian Jews by the Nazis, which although it did not have a direct influence on the massacres of 1943, indirectly contributed to the terrible devaluation of human life in the consciousness of many Volhynians.[13]

Viatrovych is well-justified in raising these issues; but in his book, he shows little genuine interest in developing them. He is more concerned with presenting a counter-argument that lacks nuance and is clearly *parti-pris* or preconceived. For example, in the preface he states that one of the lessons of the war should be that "in such conflicts it is often impossible to clearly separate participants into heroes and criminals, executioners and victims, and even less possible to draw this line between national communities that opposed one another."[14] This is a valid insight that might have been followed by information about the biographies and personal motivation of individual participants, and an analysis of what drove ordinary people to kill defenseless populations. Unfortunately, such a psychological and social analysis is not attempted.

Andriy Zayarnyuk has suggested that this kind of analysis should be the next stage in scholarly research into the events in Volhynia in 1943 and similar mass killings in the years that followed. He recommends in this connection that researchers pursue insights into violence made by Holocaust scholars, such as Raul Hilberg, Hannah Arendt, Christopher Browning, and Daniel Goldhagen.[15] Zayarnyuk also points out that the debate between "functionalists" (those, like Browning, who sought explanations for the behavior of ordinary people in a wide range of causes) and "intentionalists"

---

[13] Iaroslav Hrytsak, "Nashe i duzhe nashe hore," *Krytyka* 7–8 (2003): 7–8; quoted in Viatrovych, *Druha pols'ko-ukrains'ka viina*, 40–41.
[14] *Ibid.*, 8.
[15] Andrii Zaiarniuk, "Vykonavtsi etnichnoi chystky poliakiv na Volyni iak intelektual'na problema," *Historians.in.ua,* 8 August 2016, http://www.historians.in.ua/index.php/en/doslidzhennya/1963-andrii-zaiarniuk-vykonavtsi-etnichnoi-chystky-poliakiv-na-volyni-iak-intelektualna-problema-chastyna-1 (accessed 6 April 2018).

(those, like Goldhagen, who found explanations for violence in ideology) has strong implications for studies of the Volhynian events and could potentially enable the exploration of these events in much greater depth. It is clear, for example, that Grzegorz Rossoliński-Liebe, while he may not make this explicit, argues an "intentionalist" case when he emphasizes "the racist roots of the OUN(B) ideology" and its connection to "pathological sadism."[16] The numerous atrocities against Poles were, according to this view, ideologically motivated, planned, and ordered.[17] A more "functionalist" view that sees events as a product of the wartime situation has been presented by Timothy Snyder.[18]

The main criticisms of Viatrovych's text have focused overwhelmingly on the author's preconceived viewpoint, which produces a strongly slanted presentation of facts. In such critiques, Viatrovych's work has often been contextualized as part of the state-sponsored campaign to create heroes out of the OUN and UPA during Yushchenko's presidency (2005–2010), at a time when Viatrovych, as head of the security archives, had privileged access to materials which he could select to support his case. Similar criticisms continue to be leveled against Viatrovych today. As director of the Institute for National Memory, Viatrovych is frequently charged with waging a campaign to deny the OUN's complicity in crimes during the Second World War.[19] In the light of his expressed desire to shape cultural memory and produce a national narrative in which the OUN and UPA figure as liberation fighters, most Western scholars have questioned the author's presentation of facts. These

---

[16] Grzegorz Rossoliński-Liebe, *Stepan Bandera: The Life and Afterlife of a Ukrainian Nationalist: Fascism, Genocide, and Cult* (Stuttgart: ibidem, 2014), 268.

[17] Ibid., 268–69.

[18] Timothy Snyder, "'To Resolve the Ukrainian Problem Once and For All': The Ethnic Cleansing of Ukrainians in Poland 1943-1947," *Cold War Studies 1*, no. 2 (1999): 86–120; idem, "The Causes of Ukrainian-Polish Ethnic Cleansing 1943," *Past and Present* 179, no. 1 (2003): 197–234; and idem *The Reconstruction of Nations: Poland, Ukraine, Lithuania, Belarus, 1569–1999* (New Haven, CT: Yale University Press, 2003), 154–78.

[19] More recently, on the occasion of the President of Israel's speech in the Ukrainian parliament on 27 September 2016, Viatrovych offered a Facebook post that denied the OUN's participation in the Holocaust.

complaints were prominent in the discussion conducted in *Ab Imperio* 1 (2012).

It should be noted that not only Western scholars, but writers and political commentators in Ukraine have also complained about the use of the events in Volhynia in 1943 by political parties to promote themselves. The prominent journalist Vitaliy Portnikov has argued that the intervention of politicians into the discussion has prevented broader comparisons between similarly violent events in different places and among different peoples.[20] The writer Yurii Vynnychuk has poured scorn on the campaign by the Svoboda party to create a cult of the UPA—one that involves wearing uniforms, marching in processions, popularizing symbols never in fact used by the UPA, revering Bandera, and celebrating the feast of Mary the Protectress (Pokrova) as the day on which the UPA was supposed to have been founded. In Vynnychuk's view, "professional patriots" with a perverted understanding of historical events have influenced the public mind.[21] Taras Vozniak, the long-time editor of the L'viv journal *I*, has similarly complained of the Ukrainian public's preparedness to discuss the Volhynian massacres and the works on this subject by Polish historian Grzegorz Motyka without any knowledge of the literature on the subject and with a purely imagined idea of what Motyka's texts actually say.[22] In various articles on the topic, these authors have lamented the manipulation of the Volhynia issue by Ukrainian, Polish, and Russian presses and politicians.[23]

---

[20] Vitaliy Portnikov, "Poland and Politics: Why Politicians Should Not Meddle in History," *Euromaidan Press*, 3 September 2016, http://euromaidanpress.com/2016/09/03/poland-and-political-gains-why-politicians-should-not-meddle-in-history/#arvlbdata (accessed 6 April 2018).

[21] Iurii Vynnychuk, "Ihry profesiinykh patriotiv," in Iurii Vynnychuk *et al.* (eds.) *2014: Khronika goda: Blogi, Kolonki, Dnevniki* (Kharkiv: Folio, 2015), 338–39.

[22] Taras Vozniak, "Znovu pro Volyn' 1943 roku," in his *Retrospektyvna politolohiia: Epokha Ianukovycha—Ahoniia rezhymu* (L'viv: "I," 2014), 77.

[23] See especially Taras Vozniak's articles and interviews in Polish and Ukrainian newspapers, "Przezyc Wolyn," in his *Retrospektyvna politolohiia: Epokha Ianukovycha—Ahoniia rezhymu* (L'viv: "I," 2015), 89–94; "Volyn 1943. Pidsumky 2013. Vid potraktuvannia Volyns'koi trahedii mozhe zalezhaty pidpysannia uhody z ES," in his *Retrospektyvna politolohiia*, 95–104; and "Znovu pro Volyn' 1943 roku," in his *Retrospektyvna politolohiia*, 77–78.

Given his prominence in this debate, it is worth taking a closer look at the most vigorous scholarly complaints that have been issued against Viatrovych. In the remainder of the article, I address each of these complaints in turn, setting out to evaluate their validity and summarizing the scholarly discussion on these issues.

## 1. The issue of equivalence

The main argument put forward in Viatrovych's book is that the wartime Polish–Ukrainian conflict should be seen as part of an extended conflict, one that includes the armed clashes of 1918–19 and the confrontations within interwar Poland, the events in Chełm/Kholm in the years 1942–47, and Operation Vistula (Akcja Wisła) in 1947. These provide the wider contextualization for the Volhynian events of 1943–44. In presenting this case the author highlights atrocities that took place on the Polish side and the biased presentation of these events in the Polish media. This position, which insists on equivalence between the killing of Poles in Volhynia and the killing of Ukrainians, has been criticised widely, especially by Polish historians.

Polish scholars have refused to accept that the earlier events in Chełm/Kholm directly influenced the Volhynian massacre. They generally deny genocidal intent on the part of Polish actors, although the massacres in the villages of Piskorowice (Pyskovorychi in Ukrainian) near Rzeszów, Pawłokoma (Pavlokoma) near Przemyśl, and Werchowyna (Verkhovyna) in the Lublin Voivodeship, about which considerable evidence has been gathered, might be viewed as exceptions. Apparently without exception they reject the argument for equivalence. According to Grzegorz Motyka, the number of Poles killed in Volhynia may have been 50,000–60,000 and the number of Ukrainians 2,000–3,000. The same historian has estimated that altogether, during the years 1943–47, 80,000–100,000 Poles and 10,000–20,000 were killed in the Polish-Ukrainian conflict, while over a million Poles and 630,000 Ukrainians and Lemkos were displaced.[24] It is pointed out that the majority of Poles were civilians murdered in Volhynia in 1943. Viatrovych, by contrast, suggests that the respective figures for Polish and Ukrainian deaths might be closer to 39,000 and 16,000.[25] The attacks on Ukrainians in Chełm/Kholm in 1942–43, however brutal, it is argued, were therefore not on the same scale or of the same nature.[26] Viatrovych counters this argument by focusing on the elimination of Ukrainian community leaders, providing the figure of 543 murders of prominent figures, including priests, in the Chełm/Kholm region between August 1942 and August 1943.[27] Although Polish commentators have used the argument that these were German collaborators, it has been pointed out by several scholars, firstly, that there was a deliberate Polish policy to remove Ukrainian community leaders, and, secondly, that killing individuals from another group has always been easier than killing collaborators from one's own group.[28] The removal of elites, which was, of course, also practiced at the time by the Germans and Soviets, accelerated a rapid descent into chaos.[29]

Viatrovych makes the point that news of events in Chełm/Kholm, Galicia, and Volhynia spread rapidly between these territories, often in the form of unsubstantiated rumors, and fueled anger and violence.[30] The widespread destruction of churches and Ukrainian community life had already been initiated by the pre-war Polish authorities in 1938.[31] He argues therefore that the events of 1942–44 produced a "domino effect" in a population already aware of previous atrocities. Accordingly, "news of anti-Ukrainian actions in the Chełm/Kholm region arrived in Volhynia and provoked mass anti-Polish actions there, news of which then drove the Polish

---

[24] Grzegorz Motyka, "Zapomnijcie o Giedroyciu: Polacy, Ukraińcy, IPN," *Gazeta Wyborcza*, 24 May 2008. Recent Polish newspaper articles, however, have placed the numer of Polish victims at over twice this figure.
[25] Viatrovych, *Druha pols'ko-ukrains'ka viina*, 241–42.
[26] Gzhegozh [Grzegorz] Motyka, "Neudachnaia kniga," *Ab Imperio*, no. 1 (2012): 395–97.
[27] Viatrovych, *Druha pols'ko-ukrains'ka viina*, 126, 128.
[28] Ibid., 101, 86.
[29] Ibid., 98.
[30] Ibid., 129, 131, 140.
[31] Ibid., 86.

underground in Galicia to conduct anti-Ukrainian acts."[32] However, there is a weakness in Viatrovych's argumentation. Even though it can be accepted that these events contributed to the Ukrainian victimization narrative and the population's radicalization, they still do not explain how mass violence was triggered in Volhynia or how a decision was taken there to conduct ethnic cleansing.

## 2. Conflation of the national liberation struggle with the OUN(b), and misrepresentation of program, ideology and actions in the 1930s and early 1940s

One of Viatrovych's strongest biases is expressed through his evident desire to present the OUN as a liberation force, while ignoring any contradictory arguments. From the beginning to the end of his book he conflates the national liberation struggle not merely with the OUN but specifically with the OUN(b), that is with the Bandera faction of the organization. In fact, throughout the book, Viatrovych uses the term "national liberationists" as a synonym for the OUN(b). This is unwarranted, if only because the OUN was a minority party in the 1930s, even in Galicia. It gained control over the underground and the UPA in 1943, often through force, and even then, the fighters did not necessarily belong to the party. The term "banderites" was used as shorthand, mainly by hostile forces, for all militant nationalists in the underground. Later, in emigration the OUN(b) remained a minority party and was largely shunned and openly criticized by most Ukrainians. This was certainly the case for those who came from Central and Eastern Ukraine, but it was also the case for most intellectuals. None of this appears to interest or concern Viatrovych, which is surprising since one would expect that any discussion of the OUN as a national liberationist movement ought to take into account the views of the OUN's founders, ideologists, and leaders. In fact, most of these broke with the OUN(b) and criticized it, during and after the war.[33]

---

[32] Ibid., 181.
[33] For a brief discussion of the postwar debates within the different wings of the OUN, see Myroslav Shkandrij, *Ukrainian Nationalism: Politics, Ideology, and*

Viatrovych's text can therefore be seen as representing a contemporary defense of the OUN(b), and its policies and practices. An analysis of the book's argumentation reveals a strategy which we might label as one of "containment": acts of violence are not denied (to his credit, the author brings to light some shocking incidents), but are framed as the inevitable consequence of war and the struggle for national liberation. Violence is attributed to uncontrolled peasant groups and to a brutality representing the tenor of the time. He speaks of the constant struggle for controlling the land and opposing dominant ruling groups as a widely-observed process, and suggests (incorrectly) that scholars like Andrea Graziosi and Ernest Gellner have recognized the necessity of population removal in this region at the time.[34] He then comes close to supporting the idea of ethnic cleansing, arguing that the removal of the Polish population from Volhynia was necessary because the "Poles of Western Ukraine gave their underground personnel material and informational resources, without which their development in an ethnically foreign and often hostile terrain would have been impossible."[35]

In line with this general strategy, Viatrovych refuses to define the OUN's prewar politics or ideology, which even a cursory survey reveals to be totalitarian, anti-democratic, and sectarian. The OUN's campaign of intimidation against democratic parties and intellectuals, which accelerated under Bandera's leadership in the Galician underground during the 1930s, is ignored, and its position as a minority party in the national movement is never mentioned. Moreover, the OUN(b)'s break from the mainstream OUN leadership in Europe in 1939 and its murder of activists who refused to align themselves with the Bandera wing (in particular, those who recognized the Melnyk wing and the older European leadership) is also passed over in silence. The result is a conjurer's trick: the previous history

---

*Literature, 1929-1956* (New Haven and London: Yale University Press, 2015), 72–76, 128–31. Viatrovych's book also ignores the large body of creative literature produced by writers who were sympathetic to or members of the OUN. Most of them severely criticized the policies and action of the OUN(b). For an analysis of seven major figures, see Shkandrij, *Ukrainian Nationalism*, 175–267.

34 Viatrovych, *Druha pols'ko-ukrains'ka viina*, 43, 123.
35 Ibid., 120.

of the OUN disappears, as does awareness that there were other strands of the OUN. The impression is created of a seamless, single party under one leader. Even the acronyms OUN(b), OUN(m), or the later OUN(z) are never mentioned.

By taking such a preordained position the researcher is driven to distort facts. One example will have to suffice. In discussing the new "foreign-relations policy" produced in December 1940 by the "newly-created OUN under Stepan Bandera," Viatrovych provides a quotation from the organization's new "Manifesto." He mentions the desire expressed in this document to create "a new order" and to "lay the foundations of a political system." He then goes on to state that one of the creators of this new concept was Ivan Mitrynga, who suggested the slogan: "Together with the Poles, French, and the peoples of the USSR for a free Europe without Hitler and Stalin."[36] He fails to mention, however, that during this conference of the OUN(b) held in Krakow in February 1940, Bandera's circle rejected the slogan, saying that the search for "friends" (meaning allied peoples) was over and that "Ukraine's place was in the new Europe."[37] This new Europe was, of course, a fascist, pro-German one.

Such a blatant misrepresentation of the OUN's positions is problematic not only because it is a form of disinformation and miseducation. In the present circumstances it represents a lost opportunity to educate the public about the evolution of the OUN and UPA. Instead, the author chooses to mythologize the party and movement. However, even in terms of the desire to strengthen support for national liberationism, this is a failing strategy. Andreas Umland has argued that glorifying Bandera and the OUN is not only bad history, but ultimately damages Ukraine's reputation among its friends in the West.[38] The facts will nonetheless inevitably emerge, and will no doubt result in the eventual disillusionment of the public, when it realizes that it has been misled. A range of German,

---

[36] Viatrovych, *Druha pols'ko-ukrains'ka viina*, 73.
[37] Anatolii Kentii, *Zbroinyi chyn ukrains'kykh natsionalistiv, 1920–1956: Istoryko-arkhivni narysy*, vol. 1 (Kyiv: Derzhavnyi komitet arkhiviv Ukrainy, 2005), 180.
[38] Andreas Umland, "Bad History Doesn't Make Friends," *Foreign Policy*, 25 October 2016, https://foreignpolicy.com/2016/10/25/bad-history-doesnt-make-friends-kiev-ukraine-stepan-bandera (accessed 6 April 2018).

Polish, Ukrainian, and North American scholars have recently been producing accounts that document the activities of the OUN and UPA and paint an entirely different picture.[39] Viatrovych's evasiveness in this context represents a disservice to serious readers who wish to understand the nature of the OUN, the UPA, and the events in Volhynia during 1943-44. A reader of his book will, for example, remain unaware of the fact that the OUN's secret police, the SB, shot members of rival Ukrainian organizations, Ukrainian peasants whom it accused of various transgressions, and (in their hundreds) UPA members whom it (wrongly) suspected of disloyalty.[40]

## 3. The lack of discussion concerning the Holocaust

The book lacks any discussion of the Holocaust. It mentions in passing that the number of soldiers in the UPA was substantially strengthened when Ukrainians in the German-organized police force were given orders by the OUN to desert and join the fighters in the forest in March 1943. Viatrovych agrees that at this point the OUN-controlled UPA became the dominant underground in Volhynia, changing the balance of power.[41] However, he challenges Snyder's view that when the Germans organized a genocide of Volhynian Jews, these Ukrainian policemen had witnessed or participated in it, thus acquiring practical knowledge of how genocide can be conducted effectively.[42] Although Viatrovych claims that Snyder fails to produce any evidence, he provides no effective counter-argument to Snyder's view that the scale on which the massacre of Poles in Volhynia was conducted, its organized and coordinated nature, and its effectiveness are indications of prior knowledge of the methods of mass murder.

---

[39] Authors who have produced monographs dealing with the OUN and UPA include Frank Golczewski, Franziska Bruder, Grzegorz Motyka, Roman Wysocki, Ihor Il'iushyn, Oleksandr Zaitsev, and Grzegorz Rossoliński-Liebe.
[40] See: Karel C. Berkhoff, *Harvest of Despair: Life and Death in Ukraine under Nazi Rule* (Cambridge, MA: Belknap Press for Harvard University Press, 2004), 297.
[41] Viatrovych, *Druha pols'ko-ukrains'ka viina*, 141.
[42] Snyder, "Causes of Ukrainian–Polish Ethnic Cleansing 1943," 198–99.

In a similar way, Viatrovych denies the OUN(b)'s racism. He rejects the claim that one of the most racist publications of the late 1930s, Mykhailo Kolodzinskyi's "Voienna doktryna ukrains'kykh natsionalistiv" (Military Doctrine of Ukrainian Nationalists, 1938) had any currency within the organization. In this text Kolodzinskyi calls for a struggle not only against the state structure of the Polish occupying power, but against the people on whom it rests. They have to be "cleaned out of Ukraine as a foreign, hostile element."[43] Oleksandr Zaitsev agrees with Viatrovych that Kolodzinskyi's statements had no official support within the OUN leadership.[44] These remarks were, however, symptomatic of a drift toward greater anti-Semitic and racist positions in the years 1937–41. There is plenty of direct evidence for this in the pronouncements of the OUN(b) leaders.[45] It is also significant, as Berkhoff has pointed out, that the OUN "never opposed specifically the murder of Jews, not even in words."[46]

4. **The refusal to admit that the OUN(b) and UPA took a decision to begin the destruction of Poles in Volhynia in 1943**

The refusal to accept that any decision was made by the leadership of the OUN or the UPA to unleash the mass killing of Poles in 1943 hinges on the lack of a "smoking gun" document. Serhii Riabenko has supported Viatrovych's position here by indicating the lack of conclusive evidence in Polish accounts.[47] However, not only most Western scholars, but leading Ukrainian researchers in this field have taken a different view. Yaroslav Hrytsak, for example, has argued that a document ordering the action will probably never be

---

[43] Quoted in Viatrovych, *Druha pols'ko-ukrains'ka viina*, 52.
[44] Zaitsev indicates that Kolodzinskyi's brochure, although written in 1938, was only reproduced in 1940 in a mimeographed version, even then only a quarter of the text was included. See Oleksandr Zaitsev, *Ukrains'kyi intehral'nyi natsionalizm (1920-1930-ti roky): Narys intellektual'noi istorii* (Kyiv: Krytyka, 2016), 61–62, 318.
[45] See, for example, Shkandrij, *Ukrainian Nationalism*, 53–55, 112–21.
[46] Berkhoff, *Harvest of Despair*, 310.
[47] Riabenko, "'Druzhe Ruban!'"

found (at least not one that is unequivocal and capable of convincing everyone of its authenticity) because the instructions may well have been verbal. He is convinced, however, that such instructions were given.[48] Mykola Lebed' confided several times to his closest circle that such instructions were given by the UPA and OUN(b) leadership:

> Probably, the decision was taken by a section of the leadership, which wanted to secure its positions in the newly-created Army, and in particular to squeeze out Mykola Lebed' from the leadership. In any case, it appears that the anti-Polish action became an important factor in the creation of the UPA, its "baptism by blood." According to the norms of international law this was a war crime, from the military-political point of view it was completely senseless; after all, the decisive role in the ethnic cleansing of Poles from Volhynia and Galicia was played not by the UPA's actions but by Stalin's decisions and his agreement with his allies at Yalta.[49]

Similarly, the most authoritative Ukrainian researcher on the subject, Ihor Il'iushyn, has commented that there were many calls from community leaders to stop the violence, that the armed groups were at first under the OUN(b)'s command, and that "the anti-Polish attacks began under its orders."[50]

In fact, Viatrovych is ambivalent on this point. He places the blame on Klym Savur (Dmytro Kliachkivs'kyi), the local UPA commander in Volhynia, who "ceased to subordinate himself to the central command."[51] Kliachkivs'kyi "approved the decision to let the UPA units conduct anti-Polish actions. In his decisions he relied on a personal understanding of the situation, more than the instructions of central authorities, who, he felt, did not understand the real situation."[52] The blame therefore rests not with the center.

---

[48] Iaroslav Hrytsak, *Strasti za natsionalizmom: Istorychni ese* (Kyiv: Krytyka, 2006), 104.
[49] Ibid.
[50] I. I. Il'iushyn, *Ukrains'ka Povstans'ka Armiia i Armiia Kraiova: Protystoiannia v Zakhidniy Ukraini (1939–1945 rr.)* (Kyiv: Kyievo-Mohylians'ka Akademiia, 2009), 23, 30–32.
[51] Viatrovych, *Druha pols'ko-ukrains'ka viina*, 142.
[52] Ibid., 143.

Viatrovych does not explain why the center in any case went along with the action in subsequent weeks and months.

## 5. Reluctance to recognize the guilt of Ukrainians in conducting the massacres

Viatrovych shows a reluctance to ascribe any guilt to the Ukrainian side in the conflict, and again, frequently uses the argument of equivalency to deflect the accusation of guilt. He reasons that if it was in fact a war, with roughly equal numbers killed on both sides, one party cannot be viewed as more guilty than the other. He minimizes, obscures, or ignores assessments made by a number of prominent historians, such as Timothy Snyder and Jan T. Gross, by leading Polish scholars in the field such as Grzegorz Motyka, and by respected Ukrainian historians such as Ihor Il'iushyn and Oleksandr Zaitsev.

Viatrovych frequently distorts the arguments of other scholars, whom he tends to consider as opponents rather than interlocutors. He manifests a remarkable deafness to nuance, and sometimes an unsure handling of the secondary literature. Partially this may be due to his imperfect knowledge of other languages, but it is more convincingly attributed to a polemical intent He tends to simplify or willfully misinterpret the argument of others, as Motyka has indicated, in the manner of a debater out to score points, by accusing them of zealotry, while seemingly unaware of his own much greater zealotry in defending or glorifying the OUN.[53]

Other Ukrainian historians have responded differently. Il'iushyn has suggested that the OUN(b) leadership and the Ukrainian population that predominated in Volhynia bear the burden of responsibility for the Volhynian tragedy, in the same way as the responsibility for ethnic cleansing of Ukrainians west of the Curzon line (in Chełm, Podlachie, Nadsianie and the Lemko region) lies with the majority Polish population.[54] Yaroslav Dashkevych has commented: "the Ukrainian terror of 1942–44 against the Polish

---

[53] Motyka, "Neudachnaia kniga": 388.
[54] Il'iushyn, Ukrains'ka Povstans'ka Armiia i Armiia Kraiova, 22.

population of Western Ukraine, even after attempts to justify it by invoking the idea of revenge for Polish injustices, German and Russian provocations, collaboration by the Armia Krajowa [the Polish underground army] with communist Russia, etc., still deserves a severe and unqualified condemnation."[55]

These weaknesses in Viatrovych's overall conceptualization are compensated to a degree by the wealth of information that he offers on the details of local campaigns. The realities of the campaign to cleanse Poles from Volhynia in 1943 and the later campaigns to cleanse Ukrainians from Chełm/Kholm and other predominantly Ukrainian territories that ended up in Poland after the war are often presented in vivid detail. The information is based on materials culled from the archives and includes accounts of Polish atrocities (by troops of the Armia Krajowa, the Polish police in German service, and the postwar Polish government). Although these accounts are less forthcoming when they concern atrocities by Ukrainian forces, the inclusion of archival materials from Ukrainian sources dealing with the UPA and OUN, especially the discussion of interrogation protocols of arrested fighters, represents a welcome addition to the scholarship. Viatrovych uses these Soviet protocols effectively, demonstrating how valuable they can be, when analyzed carefully.

## 6. The issue of ethnic cleansing and genocide

Viatrovych's account is also valuable in the challenge it poses to some calcified opinions, especially concerning the use of the term genocide in discussions of the Volhynian massacres. In fact, as we have seen, he indirectly admits that ethnic cleansing occurred. His strategy is to situate the events of 1943 within the longer continuum and to cite mitigating circumstances: the wartime events in Volhynia; the Polish government's anti-Ukrainian policies of the 1930s, which included resettlement, church closures, and forcing people to declare themselves Poles; the attacks by Poles on the

---

[55] Yaroslav Dashkevych, *Ukraina vchora i nyni: Narysy, vystupy, ese: Do Druhoi mizhnarodnoi konferentsii ukrainistiv* (Kyiv: B.v., 1993), 130–31.

Ukrainian population of Chełm/Kholm in 1938 and 1941–42, and the mass deportations of 1947 during Akcja Wisła (Operation Vistula)—all of which are presented as the background against which the Volhynian massacres of 1943–44 must be viewed. Ethnic cleansing, in other words, was being practiced by the Poles and other governments at the time. Seen in this light the Volhynian massacre (or tragedy, as it is sometimes called) was a "war within a war," one that had gone on for decades and had developed its own dynamic. This is Viatrovych's "functionalist" response to the argument of "intentionalists" that the OUN had a calculated, racist intent. The new narrative represents his reconceptualization of the events in Volhynia and is his major contribution to the debate.

Nonetheless, he rejects use of the term genocide. Viatrovych cites the statement of an early Polish researcher Ryszard Torzecki, who commented that the

> leadership of the OUN wanted to remove the Polish population from these lands, since they viewed them as a hindrance in the creation of a Ukrainian state. However, they did not plan its [this population's] physical destruction. This type of action was often a spontaneous reaction of the masses and of local commanders. In many cases the actions escaped the control of the UPA. In other cases the leaders did not know how or, and this should be stressed, did not wish to control them.[56]

Viatrovych repeats this argument on several occasions. It is another way of avoiding the blame being placed on the OUN and UPA leadership. Instead, the atrocities are attributed to a peasant *jacquerie*. He indicates that the Homeland Executive (Galician leadership) of the OUN issued an order on 5 May 1944 to give the Polish population several days to emigrate to Polish territory. The order read: "If it refuses to obey this order, fighters should be sent in to liquidate the males, and to burn the houses and goods (to take them apart). Again we emphasize that the Poles first have to be urged to leave the territories and only liquidated after this, not the other way round."[57] Viatrovych comments that the Ukrainian insurgents were given

---

[56] Quoted in Viatrovych, *Druha pols'ko-ukrains'ka viina*, 36.
[57] Ibid., 222.

permission to liquidate the male population in the settlements that refused to leave, but then argues rather unconvincingly that "nowhere do we see instructions to completely destroy the Poles."[58]

As for incidents where atrocities took place, Viatrovych places the blame on renegade commanders who disobeyed orders. Some of these commanders were removed for unsanctioned contacts with the Germans.[59] Others, like Mykola Oliinyk, were executed for similar offences or for ordering the Polish population to leave.[60] The general anarchy in Volhynia in early 1943 and the brutal treatment of the Polish population is blamed on the forces of Bulba-Borovets.[61] Viatrovych is also inclined to believe reports of brutality committed by the Ukrainian Waffen SS "Galicia" Division when it put down opposition in villages. He provides insights into several controversial episodes that took place, such as the shootings in the village of Huta Peniacka on 24 February 1944, indicating that a large Soviet partisan group was passing through the village at the time.[62]

There is a consistent pattern here. Every other group is responsible for atrocities, but when it comes to the OUN(b) (and the UPA forces it controlled), the violence is either minimized or explained (and effectively explained away) as the inevitable consequence of war, the brutal struggle for control of territory, and the stubborn refusal of the Poles to countenance giving up their eastern lands or to recognize Ukrainian demands for independence. The implicit argument here is that Ukrainians were faced with a stark dilemma: they had to remove the Poles or be removed by them.

## 7. The struggle over cultural memory

Viatrovych's book has been influential within Ukraine in the ongoing debates over cultural memory. The role of the OUN during the Second World War and, more broadly, of Ukrainians in military formations during this period, has been approached from different

---

[58] Ibid., 223.
[59] Ibid., 218.
[60] Ibid., 219–20.
[61] Ibid., 137.
[62] Ibid., 213, 216–17.

angles and treated with different degrees of attention. There is a discourse of Ukrainian suffering (particularly concerning Soviet soldiers, members of the nationalist underground and UPA fighters), which is evident in memoirs, novels, and films.[63] The years after independence saw the appearance of new fictional works and films dealing with the nationalist underground and the UPA. In this discourse of victimhood, the role of Ukrainians as perpetrators has not been explored. Nor has much attention been devoted to demystifying the pervasive image of victimhood by focusing on guilt and collaboration.

It is instructive to compare the German situation. Different levels of personal guilt have been an important issue in Germany since the Wehrmacht exhibition of 1996. A discourse around German guilt has opened up new approaches to understanding the experience of German soldiers during the war. Moreover, memory culture of the war is constantly undergoing change. Memory is now conceived as able to accommodate different perspectives. As it changes, it brings up aspects of history that have been previously overshadowed or forgotten. Cultural memory studies have attempted to understand how recollections are preserved over generations. This approach also recognizes that the memory of a group is related to the way it defines its identity. Aleida Assmann has described memory as tied to identity and supporting the self-image of groups.[64] However, each group deals with memory in a different manner and memory itself is an unstable phenomenon.[65] In an influential work on the subject, Michael Rothberg has further defined memory as multidirectional, as "subject to ongoing negotiations,

---

[63] Perhaps the most prominent example is Oksana Zabuzhko's novel *Muzei pokynutykh sekretiv* (Kyiv: Fakt, 2010).

[64] Aleida Assmann, "The Holocaust—A Global Memory? Extensions and Limits of a New Memory Community," in Aleida Assmann and Sebastian Konrad (eds.), *Memory in a Global Age: Discourses, Practices and Trajectories* (Basingstoke: Palgrave Macmillan, 2010), 99,

[65] Gregor Feindt, Felix Krawatzek, Daniela Mehler, Friedemann Pestel, and Ricke Trimcev, "Entangled Memory: Towards a Third Wave in Memory Studies," *History and Theory* 53, no. 1 (2014): 43.

cross-referencing and borrowing," as "productive and not private" and therefore open to "cooperation."[66]

German society has been through the *Historikerstreit* discussion of the 1980s and the Wehrmacht Exhibition debate of the 1990s.[67] This last, *Wehrmachtsausstellung* exhibition opened on 5 March 1995 and was held in thirty-three German and Austrian cities; a second revised exhibition opened in November 2001, generating much debate.[68] An influence has also been exerted by the Goldhagen–Browning debate of the later 1990s, in which Goldhagen argued the eliminationist thesis (the idea that perpetrators were driven by an eliminationist anti-Semitism), while Browning put forward the view that different factors influence people.[69] Through these discussions a broader readership is now familiar with shades of guilt (among bystanders and perpetrators), individual and shared responsibility. German guilt and suffering have coexisted in popular awareness since the 1970s, when the Holocaust memory entered the public sphere.[70]

The German experience with regard to memory politics has been influential in shaping scholarly views. However, memory politics within each country has its own complications, because various groups promote differing narratives for their own purposes. Ukrainian memory studies are presently only beginning to deal with the coexistence of different memories concerning a shared past. Victim and perpetrator memories of the Second World War have clashed,

---

[66] Michael Rothberg, *Multidirectional Memory: Remembering the Holocaust in the Age of Decolonization* (Palo Alto, CA: Stanford University Press, 1997), 3.

[67] On the former discussion see: Martin Traverse, "History Writing and the Politics of Historiography: the German Historikerstreit," *Australian Journal of Politics and History* 37, no. 2 (1991): 246–61.

[68] Hans-Gunther Thiele, *Die Wehrmachtsaussstelling: Dokumentation einer Kontroverse*, 2nd ed. (Bremen: Edition Temmen, 1999), 11–12.

[69] See: J. Daniel Goldhagen, Christopher R. Browning, and Leon Wieseltier, with an introduction by Michael Berenbaum, "The 'Willing Executioners'/ 'Ordinary Men' Debate," in *Selections from the Symposium. United States Holocaust Memorial Museum 1996*, 8 April 1996, https://www.ushmm.org/m/pdfs/Publication_OP_1996-01.pdf (accessed 6 April 2018).

[70] Aleida Assmann, "On the (In) Compatibility of Guilt and Suffering in German Memory," trans. Linda Shoru, *German Life and Letters* 59(2) (2006): 187, http://dx.doi.org/10.1111/j.0016-8777.2006.00344.x (accessed 6 April 2018).

perhaps nowhere more than in accounts of the OUN and the Volhynian massacres. The myth of the innocent fighter or young person caught up in the war, while not necessarily false, has to be set against the much greater victimhood of civilian populations, particularly Jews, but also, in the case of Volhynia, Poles. As awareness of these events has grown, this has drawn attention to the coexistence of both victimhood and perpetratorship in one group or person.

This complex reality has to confront the general tenor of current debates, in which the OUN and the UPA are viewed by some commentators as outright guilty parties without the right to inclusion in a narrative of suffering, and by others as unquestionably heroic organizations with no relationship to perpetratorship. Such a juxtaposition of simplified positions in the mass media has now reached a sterile impasse. It does not allow discussion of other questions, such as the effects of the devastation caused by the war, the circumstances that brought about recruitment to armed groups, the psychology of those who participated in violent acts, and the role of unwilling or underage participants. Viatrovych's text has to some degree encouraged this narrative simplification and sharpening of views.

On the other hand, however, the scholarly debate around the book has identified tensions between competing memory groups and demonstrated the ways in which history can be put to political uses. This debate has also made clear that the German reconciliation experience was conducted under different circumstances, and was based on historical assumptions that no longer enjoy universal acceptance. The debate today is being conducted in a much more challenging international reality, against the backdrop of the war with Russia, the appearance of far-right parties and governments throughout Europe, the rise of aggressive populisms, the use of disinformation as a way of undermining civil society, and the manipulation of media to cause internal conflict. The belief in a stable Europe, consensual politics, even democratic values, is now increasingly challenged. In this respect Viatrovych's text is a reflection of the aggressive tone in which public debates are being conducted.

## 8. An argument for recognizing complexity

There is no question among historians that the Ukrainian population was victimized during and after the war. Tarik Cyril Amar has written that after reoccupying Western Ukraine, the Soviet party-state "won its dirty war of counterinsurgency, killing more than 150,000, deporting more than 200,000, and incarcerating nearly 110,000 locals."[71] In Poland under Operation Vistula, which began on 28 April 1947, some 150,000 Ukrainians were deported from the country's south-eastern lands by the Polish army in cooperation with Soviet forces. These brutal operations led to the forcible removal and dispersal of Ukrainian populations and to the final crushing of the UPA. Operation Vistula has been viewed by many as an act of revenge for the removal of Poles from Volhynia.[72]

However, the experience of Ukrainian victimhood has not often been described in Ukrainian scholarship and literature alongside the victimhood of Poles, Jews, and others. The problem here is how to design an overarching narrative. A narrative that goes beyond simple fables and myths must integrate complicated questions.

Among such questions is the wartime cooperation of Ukrainian organizations. For example, the Ukrainian Central Committteee (*Ukrainskyi Tsentral'nyi Komitet* or UTsK) has never been properly studied and analyzed. It worked with the Germans. Amar describes this as "a form of collaboration *afin d'état*, an attempt to instrumentalize Nazi power for Ukrainian national aims, including the creation of a state."[73] However, this is a gross simplification of the Committeee's work, which often involved attempts to alleviate the plight of Ukrainian victims of the war, including children, prisoners-of-war, the wounded, hungry, and destitute. The struggle to keep basic schooling and social services operating in the midst of wartime devastation cannot be construed simply as instrumentalizing German rule.

---

[71] Tarik Cyril Amar, *The Paradox of Lviv: A Borderland City between Stalinists, Nazis, and Nationalists* (Ithaca and London: Cornell University Press, 2015), 17.
[72] Viatrovych, *Druha pols'ko-ukrains'ka viina*, 296–97.
[73] Amar, *Paradox of Lviv*, 128.

On the other side of the ledger lie under-researched issues of complicity in violence, such as the problem of postwar killings by nationalists, primarily by the OUN(b) and UPA under its control. The number of such killings has been estimated at 30,676; half were peasant and collective-farm members.[74] The emerging overall picture is of a complex interaction between various contradictory tendencies (the drive for national liberation, the temptation to collaborate, and the repeated victimization of local populations). The story of the interaction of these tendencies has in fact never been told in the Ukrainian context.

In his classic study *Ordinary Men* Christopher Browning demonstrates how mass murder and routine can become normal, and how in hindsight memory presents a confusing array of perspectives.[75] He describes, for example, how in 1942–43 Jew–hunting in the countryside was part of the work done by the Order Police *(Ordnungspolizei)*, but how this was never reported in interviews conducted with this police.[76] He similarly describes how German policemen when interviewed shifted the blame for anti-Semitism onto local Poles.[77] Browning emphasizes the impact of systematic destruction on the people who witnessed it or participated in it, and the importance of social influences in allowing individuals to commit atrocities.[78] The potential for violence, he suggests, can under particular circumstances be roused in all people, who at a later date can revert to law-abiding behavior.[79] Although ideological indoctrination plays a role in obtaining willing obedience, Browning considers this an insufficient explanation for participation in violence.[80] Among the Order Police some individuals refused to kill, while others stopped killing at a certain point. "Human responsibility is

---

[74] P. S. Sokhan, *et al.*, *Litopys Ukrains′koi povstans′koi armii*, n.s. 7 (Toronto: Litopys UPA, 2003), 68–69; quoted in *ibid.*, 195.
[75] Christopher Browning, *Ordinary Men: Reserve Police Battalion 101 and the Final Solution in Poland* (New York: Harper Perennial, 1993), xviii–xix.
[76] *Ibid.*, 121–32.
[77] *Ibid.*, 150-55.
[78] *Ibid.*, 165-66.
[79] *Ibid.*, 166.
[80] *Ibid.*, 176, 179.

ultimately an individual matter," he concludes.[81] These considerations are germane to any analysis of the violence unleashed in Volhynia. Yet, scholarship has not explored them, and Viatrovych's book shows no interest in opening up such psychological lines of inquiry.

A scholar interested in an "intentionalist" approach (the overriding importance of national liberation in Viatrovych's case) might be expected to consider how extreme forms of violence are often motivated by principle, which acts as a higher law. The appeal of nationalism as a quasi-religious belief might profitably be investigated by the researcher, but so far has not been. Instead, the reader is left with the picture of a violent national liberation struggle, but without an understanding of why many villagers participated in the violence. To grasp this, we no doubt have to go beyond an exclusive focus on ideology.

The complex experience of local people is probably best treated as a whole, as the product of waves of violence by successive invading armies and violent regimes. First the Soviet regime, then the Germans conducted mass arrests and deportations, spread violent propaganda and recruited local people into battalions and auxiliary units. Then the process was repeated again when the Soviets returned. The primary targets of the violence were different in the various waves: initially Poles, then Jews and Russians, then Ukrainians and Poles were victims. Viatrovych's book hints at this overall picture and at times moves in the direction of such an analysis, but this exploration is then arrested by the author's polemical intent and defensive posture vis-à-vis the OUN and UPA. This makes it a provocative and interesting contribution to the debate, but, at the same time, one that is deeply flawed.

---

[81] *Ibid.*, 188.

# Correspondence

Dear Editors:

I need to register an error in a recent article in *JSPPS* that impugns my reputation. The article in question is Yaroslav Hrytsak, "Ukrainian Memory Culture Post-1991: The Case of Stepan Bandera," in *JSPPS*, 2017, no. 2.

Professor Hrytsak, referring to my article on the Lviv pogrom of July 1941 that appeared in *Canadian Slavonic Papers* in 2011, wrote the following: "The documents proving the participation of Ukrainian police in the pogrom were uncovered by American scholar Jeffrey Burds; he passed them to John-Paul Himka, who published them without Burds' permission, leading the latter to accuse Himka of plagiarism in the course of a heated discussion on Facebook" (Hrytsak, p. 194, n. 33.)

I need to clarify this. Jeffrey Burds did once share with me materials on the role of the Ukrainian nationalists in the pogrom, for which I remain very grateful. They were not documents per se, but photographs. For my article on the Lviv pogrom, I found many other photos and films held by Yad Vashem, the United States Holocaust Memorial Museum, and others that recorded the involvement of the militia (not police) of the Organization of Ukrainian Nationalists (OUN) in the pogrom. Of the photos Professor Burds originally shared with me, some came from the Wiener Library in London. I independently contacted Wiener Library to obtain a full set of their Lviv pogrom photos and acquired permission to reproduce some of them for the article. Other photographs came from a mutual friend, David Lee Preston. For my article on the Lviv pogrom, I examined Mr. Preston's complete collection of photos and papers relating to the Holocaust in Lviv at his office in Philadelphia and also received permission to reproduce some photos in my article. There was a third set of photos that Professor Burds shared with me, photos on militia identification papers. I had received his permission to use one in an article I published in Ukrainian a few years earlier ("Dostovirnist' svidchennia: reliatsiia Ruzi Vagner pro l'vivs'kyi pohrom vlitku 1941 r." *Holokost i suchasnist'* no. 2 (4) (2008): 43-79.)

I did not have his permission to use it for the article on the Lviv pogrom in *Canadian Slavonic Papers*, and so it does not appear there. Since then, I have received the full set of militia ID photos from elsewhere, together with permission to reproduce them. Moreover, much of the evidence I adduce in my article on the participation of the OUN militia in the pogrom comes from testimonies and memoirs, all of which I found on my own, particularly while working at the United States Holocaust Memorial Museum in 2009 and 2010.

**JOHN-PAUL HIMKA**
Professor emeritus
University of Alberta

# Reviews

Christoph Mick, *Lemberg, Lwów, L'viv, 1914–1947: Violence and Ethnicity in a Contested City*. West Lafayette, IN: Purdue University Press, 2015. xii + 458 pp.

This is an abridged and updated translation of Professor Mick's well-received monograph in German, which came out in 2011. Compared to the German edition, the author's cuts are not significant, the excised material usually covering aspects of everyday life in Lviv not immediately related to war and ethnic reordering. The English edition also features a more detailed explanation of the author's research approach, which is based on *Erfahrungsgeschichte*, or the "history of experience." Not as widely known in English-speaking academia as it is in Germany, this trend that is associated with the work of Reinhart Koselleck calls for the close study of interaction between perceptions, actions, and their interpretations as the components of the same system, which are constantly influencing each other. Mick applies this concept to the extremely complex case of the multinational city that was called Lemberg in the Habsburg Empire, Lwów in interwar Poland, and Lviv/Lvov in the postwar Soviet Union.

Mick succeeds admirably in demonstrating that it was not necessarily the war itself but, rather, the contemporary and postwar conflicts about its meaning that sealed off the new ethnic hierarchy. To be sure, World War I helped establish ethnicity as a marker of loyalty, especially in relation to Jews and Ukrainians (Ruthenians). Yet, it was the Polish-Ukrainian war of 1918–19 that became the main construction site for Polish memory and identity in Lviv. At first a strange conflict with binational committees supervising the water works and the belligerents taking breaks in the fighting to take pictures together (pp. 151–52), it soon adopted the familiar language of "atrocities" and the use of concentration camps. When the city's Jewish community declared its neutrality, the Poles saw this act as treasonous, this perception fueling a massive and violent pogrom. During the 1920s and 1930s the competing commemorative practices of *Obrona Lwowa* ("The Defense of Lviv" in Polish) and *Lystopadovyi*

*Chyn* ("The November Deed" in Ukrainian) established not just two antagonistic readings of these events, but also mutually-exclusive notions of Polishness and Ukrainianness. The city's Jews came to terms with the Polish victory by never referring in public to the pogrom—a strategy also thought to assist the healing process (pp. 233–34).

Yet, the anniversaries of the November 1918 events prompted renewed anti-Jewish violence. In a turn of events eerily foreshadowing *Kristallnacht*, in the fall of 1932 Polish student activists in Lviv called for a boycott of Jewish shops. On 12 November, when they were returning from the unveiling of a plaque dedicated to *Obrona Lwowa*, they smashed the windows of fifty-nine Jewish commercial establishments in the city center (p. 242). The Ukrainian political scene became radicalized as well. Originally established by disaffected veterans of the Ukrainian Revolution, the clandestine Organization of Ukrainian Nationalists embraced terror as a political tool. One of these Ukrainian veterans, Dmytro Paliïv, went on to establish the right-wing Front of National Unity, which even the German Embassy characterized as fascist (p. 247).

It was into this deeply polarized ethno-political scene that the Soviets arrived in the fall of 1939. Mick provides a balanced and well-informed account of their first "liberation" of Lviv, which focusses on the power of the ethnic lens. He stresses repeatedly that, in Soviet ideology, Polish domination in Eastern Galicia before 1939 was "in the first instance, social and, only in the second, national" (p. 262). Likewise, the reactions of the locals to the events in the fall of 1939 were shaped not so much by their national identification as "political and class beliefs" (p. 261). However, the local Poles and Ukrainians in particular viewed both through "ethnic patterns of perception" (p. 287). Such identification of national or religious identity with a certain kind of politics enabled the bloody ethnic conflicts of the war period, as well as the implementation of the Holocaust. Mick contrasts the Soviets' behavior in 1939 with 1944, when they, too, embraced the ethnic lens. This time around they considered the Poles as a homogenous group of nationalists and supporters of the London government-in-exile (p. 330). This logic provided the basis for the infamous "population exchanges" between the Ukrainian

SSR and Poland, which should properly be called expulsions or deportations.

As a result of the Holocaust and these events, postwar Lviv became an overwhelmingly Ukrainian city with Russians rather than Poles or Jews emerging as the largest minority. However, Mick is rightly skeptical of the Stalinist "Ukrainization" of Lviv in 1939, as well as after 1944. He argues that the Ukrainization of 1939 was, in many respects, "only external" (p. 269), but even these measures were partly scaled back in 1946, "with priority given to Sovietization" (p. 339).

Overall, this is an excellent book, which confirms that it is productive to study East European locales over a longer period of time, including both world wars. There are a few minor mistakes that should be eliminated in any subsequent editions. Khrushchev's first name was Nikita, not Mykola, which is the Ukrainian version of Nikolai (p. 265). The number of victims of the Polish–Ukrainian war (1918–19) is given as 25,000 on p. 183, but 20,000 in the table on p. 210. This reviewer is puzzled by the consistent use of "the Ukraïna" rather than the standard English "Ukraine." The Library of Congress transliteration table exempts Ukrainian and Russian place names from indicating a soft sign, which should have applied to Lviv. In any case, the soft sign should have been rendered with the prime character rather than an apostrophe.

**Serhy Yekelchyk**
University of Victoria

Tarik Cyril Amar, *The Paradox of Ukrainian Lviv: A Borderland City between Stalinists, Nazis, and Nationalists*. Ithaca, NY: Cornell University Press 2015. 368pp.

As a borderland city with a multi-ethnic legacy, Lviv is a perennial focus of scholarly attention. The twists and turns of its history, population shifts, and successive rearrangements of the urban landscape—all this constitutes a rich field for research in various disciplines. Undoubtedly, it was the twentieth century, which brought the collapse of the Russian, Ottoman, and Austro-Hungarian Empires, revolutions, and world wars, that led to the most drastic changes in the region of Central-Eastern Europe. All this was reflected in processes that took place in the city of Lviv, the profound analysis of which can certainly become a valuable contribution to scholarly exploration of the broader region.

This book by Tarik Cyril Amar is yet another study dedicated to the complicated case of Lviv. It focuses on the course of the making of modern Lviv and examines the ways in which World War II and the Soviet experience influenced and facilitated its transformation from a diverse multi-ethnic city to a predominantly Ukrainian one. In particular, Amar takes a close look at the impact of the twentieth century's key ideologies—Nazism, nationalism, and Soviet communism—on the nature of the city, local identities, and ethno-cultural diversity.

The book consists of eight chronologically organized chapters, each of which examines a particular episode in Lviv's twentieth-century history. It contains a succinct but detailed foreword which introduces and explains the main conceptual categories used by the author. The first chapter offers a brief history of the city before 1939 with special attention to inter-ethnic relations and their instrumentalization by various political actors. It gives an extensive overview of the historical background which is crucial for understanding the roots of further developments in the city during and after World War II.

Noteworthy is the fact that Amar dedicates an entire chapter to the first period of Soviet rule in Lviv (1939–41). Within less than two years the city became an object of rapid Sovietization—at that point, within the framework of the Stalinist socialist system. The implementation of Soviet nationalities policy in Lviv during the first years of World War II contributed greatly to the intensification of inter-ethnic tensions within the city. Previously, the everyday life of Lviv's Polish population in this period has been researched in depth by Grzegorz Hryciak (2000). Building upon Hryciak's study, Amar thoroughly examines Polish, Ukrainian, and Jewish encounters.

One of the book's strongest assets is the fact that Amar does not only concentrate on the two main (Polish and Ukrainian) actors in the twentieth-century disputes over Lviv, but gives plenty of attention to the often neglected Jewish history of the city. While analyzing the interplay of various ethnic and political actors in Nazi-occupied Lviv, Amar raises the controversial topic of the participation of the Organization of Ukrainian Nationalists in the Lviv pogrom of July 1941. Highlighting the most transformative episodes in Lviv's post-World War II history, the author zooms in on the closing of Lviv's last synagogue. Through this single case study, he shows the interplay between local and Soviet-wide factors in the execution of Soviet religious policy.

As Aleksandra Matyukhina (2000) demonstrated beautifully in her anthropological study of the city, Soviet nationalities policies coupled with the process of forced industrialization indeed affected the making of Ukrainian Lviv, bringing as they did rural Ukrainian culture to the city, including via the workers who carried this culture from surrounding villages. Amar takes an in-depth and comprehensive look at this issue and puts his analysis into the larger historical context. His arguments are supported by an impressive bulk of archival sources and other documents.

It is clear that, as Amar argues, Lviv took its current shape and became an utterly Ukrainian city precisely as the result of Soviet policies. The current mythologization of the city's Habsburg and multicultural past seems to be an example of what Andreas Huyssen (2003) calls "urban palimpsest": even though most of Lviv's current population does not have much in common with its pre-World War II inhabitants, previous layers of the city's history are becoming more and more noticeable over time. Today's generation of residents absorb the city's past and perceive it as their own—and as a result, the history of the city as shaped by the outcomes of Soviet policies is somewhat blurred. Ultimately, the palimpsest features of the city add to its paradoxical nature: Lviv became overwhelmingly Ukrainian as the result of its Sovietization, and yet the city has never broken irrevocably with its pre-Soviet past.

The issue of paradoxicality is flagged up in the book's title, and yet it seems to lack proper emphasis in the course of the analysis, and especially in the conclusion, which the reader would expect to be more theoretically inspired. Nevertheless, this relatively new work on Lviv's twentieth-century history is well worth reading. It steps aside from classical historicized fact-driven narration, proposing a closer examination of particularly meaningful cases instead. Well-argued, based on profound archival research and a fundamental analysis of secondary literature produced across multiple scholarly milieux, Amar's book is yet another step towards the comprehensive understanding of the complex recent history of Eastern Galicia in general, and Lviv in particular. In spite of a seemingly large existing corpus of research dedicated to Lviv, the city's recent history still lacks detailed study, and new research questions continue to emerge. This book will hopefully open the floor for further discussions and in-depth investigation of how a particular ideology may work in a single peripheral location, coupled with its own peculiarities.

**Yulia Oreshina**
PhD candidate
University of Regensburg

Victoria Khiterer, *Jewish Pogroms in Kiev During the Russian Civil War, 1918-1920*. Lewiston, New York: The Edward Mellon Press, 2015. 108 pp.

Victoria Khiterer's short monograph seeks to provide the first comprehensive account of the pogroms inflicted upon Jews in Kyiv during the Russian civil wars by Ukrainian, Russian, and Polish forces. She aims to counter the apologist historiography among latter-day supporters of both the Ukrainian nationalist and Russian White movements that downplay the leaders' responsibility by blaming the anti-Semitic violence on spontaneous acts by insubordinate rank-and-file soldiers.

More than half of the book's almost 90 pages deal with the pogroms committed by troops of the Ukrainian People's Republic (*Ukrainska narodna respublika*, hereafter UNR). This is entirely appropriate: they were responsible for about 40% of the recorded pogroms in Ukraine and more than half of the deaths. While there were a few outbreaks in Kyiv in 1917, Khiterer identifies January 1918 as a turning point: the Russian, Polish, and Jewish parties in the Ukrainian revolutionary parliament either voted against or abstained on the issue of Ukrainian independence, and, when the Bolsheviks took Kyiv that month, they stayed in the city. But only the Jews were held to collective account by the UNR troops. These now saw the whole Jewish population as inherently pro-Bolshevik and anti-Ukrainian. UNR troops perpetrated pogroms throughout the country, the worst in spring 1919. In Kyiv itself, UNR soldiers attacked Jews when they took the city alongside the Germans in March 1918, during their retreat in February 1919 and on the one day they spent in Kyiv in August 1919 (although not in December 1918 on their entry after the Germans' expulsion).

Khiterer firmly lays responsibility at the feet of Symon Petliura, commander in chief of the UNR army and, from February 1919, the Ukrainian head of state. Petliura did nothing to stop the violence or punish pogromists in his army. Moreover, argues Khiterer, he made a number of anti-Semitic statements in public and private.

Khiterer's desire to counter the exculpatory narrative that dominates Ukrainian writing on Petliura and the pogroms is entirely praiseworthy. However she does not employ the necessary sources to make a convincing argument. Khiterer asserts that the lack of surviving primary documents from the time of the pogroms means one can gain a better understanding of the violence in Kyiv using memoirs. She quotes autobiographical novels by the Soviet writers Nikolai Ostrovskii and Konstantin Paustovskii, who were in Ukraine during the civil wars. But it is unclear what here is fact and what fiction or a product of the ideological constraints placed upon those writing in the Soviet Union.

Similarly Khiterer cites Volodymyr Vynnchenko to prove that Petliura made anti-Semitic remarks in private. Certainly Vynnychenko served in government with Petliura and had numerous opportunities to hear Petliura's personal views. However, after reluctantly resigning his position, Vynnychenko devoted himself to castigating Petliura in print. Moreover, as the head of the Ukrainian government during the first major wave of pogroms, Vynnychenko had sufficient reason to find someone else to blame. He is no more a reliable witness than the Soviet authors.

Khiterer does refer to one text by Petliura—*Moskovska vosha* (Muscovite Louse), written in exile in 1925, but not published until the 1960s. This she describes as a work of "antisemitic raving" (p. 51) that reached "the same conclusion regarding national minorities in Ukraine as Nazi [sic] did in Germany" (p. 44). She even writes that "it is difficult to say if Petliura wrote his books under the influence of" (p. 44) Hitler's *Mein Kampf*. However it is unclear why she thinks it likely or even possible that Petliura could have read a book in German by a then obscure recently released prisoner that appeared in the same year as he wrote his own composition.

*Moskovska vosha* is an interesting text, and Khiterer deserves credit for rescuing it from obscurity. A couple of passages recall the canard of Judeo–Bolshevism. One points to Ukrainian Jews as the third group in Ukraine after the Russian intelligentsia and workers that supported the Muscovite invaders;[1] another claims that Jews made up 28% of the Communist Party in Ukraine (after the 65% Muscovites and Russians), concluding that "not Ukrainians but Muscovites and Jews rule" the country.[2] Jews thus appear as Ukraine's secondary enemy, helping Ukraine's main Muscovite foe, something quite typical of Ukrainian anti-Semitic thinking.

Nevertheless, for a supposedly rapidly anti-Semitic screed, Jews are remarkably absent: in over 100 pages, they only appear in three passages. The most virulent invective is reserved for Ukraine's external enemy, the Muscovites (i.e., Russians from outside Ukraine):[3] after all, the "lice" in the title are Muscovites, not Jews. The book also contained criticism of Ukrainians who did not support Petliura.[4] Shortly before his death, Petliura was probably moving toward a more anti-Semitic position, employing more explicitly than ever before the canard of Judeo–Bolshevism. But this seems to

---

[1] Symon Petliura, *Moskovska vosha. Opovidannia diadka Semena pro te, iak Moskov'ki voshi idiat Ukrainu ta shcho z nymy treba robyty* (Paris: Biblioteka im. S. Petliury i natsionalistychne vydavntstvo Evropi, 1966), 24-26.
[2] Ibid., 48.
[3] Ibid., 91.
[4] Ibid., 34-35, 41.

be part of a more general bitterness in response to his failure and exile. Consequently, it does not necessarily reflect his thinking in 1919, as Khiterer suggests. Lastly Khiterer makes the text sound more anti-Semitic by translating the Ukrainian word *zhyd* as "Yid," but it was not clear whether its use at that time indicated anti-Semitic intentions.

These source problems mean that Khiterer fails to make the case against Petliura. His latter-day admirers will dismiss her work. This is a pity, because there is a case to be made. Khiterer mentions that Petliura arrived in Zhytomyr during a pogrom. Because she does not use the published collections of archival documents, however, she misses the fact that while he was there he issued a proclamation claiming that the Ukrainian people were rising up against the "new pillager Muscovites and Jews".[5] In meetings with Jewish representatives, Petliura tied the question of Jewish safety to Jewish loyalty.[6] Yet there is other archival evidence complicating this picture. Khiterer is wrong to claim that Petliura did not condemn pogroms until August 1919. For example, he wrote several telegrams before this to local commanders calling on them to punish pogromists.[7] Thus Petliura was not a supporter of pogroms as such, but he shared some of the same prejudices as the pogromists. This explains his failure to punish the perpetrators. Countering exculpatory nationalist narratives is important, but it needs to be on the sound basis of archival sources.

**Christopher Gilley**
Durham University Library

---

[5] L. B. Miliakova *et al.* (eds.), *Kniga pogromov. Pogromy na Ukraine, v Belorussii i evropeiskoi chasti Rossii v period Grazhdanskoi voiny. 1918–1922 gg.: Sbornik dokumentov* (Moscow: Rosspen, 2008), 85.
[6] Volodymyr Serhiichuk (ed.), *Pohromy v Ukraini: 1914-1920. Shtuchnykh stereotypiv do hirkoi pravdy, prykhovuvanoi v radianskykh arkhivakh* (Kyiv: Vydavnytstvo imeni Oleny Telihy, 1999), 316-317.
[7] *Ibid.*, 198, 310-311.

Leonid Rein, *The Kings and the Pawns: Collaboration in Byelorussia during World War II*. New York: Berghahn Books, 2011. 458 pp.

Stefan Zweig was the first of many who used the game of chess to think through the dynamics of the Nazi regime. In *The Royal Game* (*Schachnovelle*, 1941), Zweig juxtaposes different styles of playing chess as personified by Mirko Czentovic, a semiliterate yet ambitious world chess champion on the one hand, and Dr. B., a man who had studied a book of chess combinations to survive while he was held in solitary confinement by the Nazi regime on the other. Widely seen as the portrayal of the workings of trauma (B.'s pain is triggered by Czentovic's cold, computed approach, and he can protect himself against it only by avoiding exposure to his past experiences in the very form of a chess game), the novella also advances Zweig's analysis of fascism as an ideology that rewards callous, calculated, and pragmatic behavior. Chess, in other words, functions to explore the psychology of social actors and relationships of power, as well as agency.

In choosing a title that references two perceived poles of power—the King representing the most powerful and the Pawn the least powerful players in the game—Rein suggests that the issue of collaboration during the German occupation of what is now the Republic of Belarus can be analyzed in these two opposing terms. His study remains one of very few to attend to local responses to, and participation in, occupation policies and violence. Despite its age and some internal problems, the monograph offers important insights that ought to motivate further inquiries. In particular, the supposedly clear division between those in power and those who are not, which Rein himself questions to some extent, requires more scholarly attention.

Overall, the monograph makes for a very slow read; its wealth of detail and the author's attempt to be as thorough as possible are at once a strength and a weakness. As a result, the author does not address the subject of the book until chapter 4. The book begins with three chapters offering a theoretical overview of studies of collaboration in Europe, the historical background of Belarusian prewar history, and a summary of German policies in the occupied

BSSR. Chapters are very uneven, ranging in length from anywhere between 26 and 72 pages, and most of them would have benefited from streamlining the argument and a sharper focus.

Most disappointing is chapter 1; the discussion of existing scholarship on collaboration falls far short of providing a strong foundation for the subsequent analysis. The chapter draws on often outdated analyses of mostly Western European societies, and it is at times contradictory. For instance, on p. 29 Rein recites Bertram Gordon's 1968 assessment that the Vichy government opposed ideological collaboration, only to state on p. 41 that "the anti-Semitic course of the Vichy regime was pursued without any pressure from the German side." Furthermore, Rein's application of the concept of economic collaboration to the work performed by foreign workers "for various German projects both within and outside Western Europe" (p. 36) is quite problematic. He includes here the labor provided by Dutch, Belgian, and French workers, the recruitment of whom "*initially at least*, proceeded on a voluntary basis" (*ibid.;* my emphasis). Where other scholars have placed this phenomenon in the framework of the exploitation of foreign, often forced labor for the German war economy, Rein's assessment denies that many Western European workers also suffered from exploitation, humiliation, and violence. The lack of nuance invites accusations against those who were often forcibly recruited for labor in the service of German companies, farms, or private households and which ruined their lives for years after the war, notably in the former Soviet Union.

In addition to these inconsistencies, the purpose of the chapter remains somewhat unclear. As the author admits, "[i]t is indeed difficult, if not senseless, to provide what purports to be an exact and all-encompassing definition of the term collaboration ... It occurred in virtually all spheres of life and was not relegated to any particular country. It affected all the countries that found themselves under Nazi rule during World War II" (p. 18). The difficulty to offer a clear definition of "collaboration" is reflected in the fact that the chapter has no conclusion and Rein does not use the overview to develop a working definition of collaboration that guides his analysis.

In some ways, this gap reflects the complexity of the situation and the difficulty to define agency in a situation of intense violence. As Rein emphasizes, why or how people collaborate with a foreign power is always dependent on concrete circumstances, overall agendas of both occupiers and occupied, and potential benefits. He therefore tries to capture the phenomenon by focusing initially on particular organizations and institutions that would seem to have clearly identifiable goals that would allow an assessment according to these categories: one chapter focuses on efforts to "build" a state through self-help and youth organizations that reflect the aims of the national movements of the 1920s; the following chapter on the relationship of the Belorussian Orthodox Church to the occupation authorities; and another on the role of the "official" Belorussian press.

Only the last two chapters before the conclusion turn to the participation of individuals in institutions and organizations created by the occupation regime: people who volunteered or were recruited for local police battalions, which, among others, participated in the mass murder of Jews, or others who contributed to the German military effort. In relative terms—compared, for instance, to Lithuanian or Latvian responses of this kind—few local non-Jews participated. In part, and as Rein argues, this reflects the German view of Belarusians as racially inferior beings who were incapable of helping to implement the New European Order prescribed by Nazi ideology. Other scholars suggest that the lack of a strong Belarusian national movement limited the number of those who may have hoped to use the German occupation regime to fulfill anti-Soviet or nationalist aspirations (which was ill-fated elsewhere too but did motivate organizations such as the UPA). The brutality of German violence against Jews and non-Jewish residents seems to have further limited enthusiasm among locals to join, and local lore continues to describe the choices people had as either joining the police or being transported to forced labor. In essence, both the scale and the motivation to join the occupying forces in, for instance, the implementation of the Holocaust remain unclear and require further research.

Rein relies in his analysis of German occupation policy and Belorussian collaboration on literature published before early 2002, as well as on German and Belorussian documentation that was available to him in the form of copies stored at Yad Vashem Archives. The book's scope is therefore somewhat limited and offers little to trace the perspective of those considered collaborators themselves or to illuminate how or why locals responded in particular ways. Scholars like Tanja Penter, Franziska Exeler, and Alana Holland are using archival material based on Soviet war crime trials and a number of other sources to access these elements. Similarly, oral histories and other research conducted by scholars based in Belarus since the late 1990s promise further insight into the concrete local and personal dynamics of collaboration and will help untangle the web of different responses.

Again, Rein delivers important insights drawing on a limited source base and his work ought to be seen as a stimulant for further research. He rejects the idea that collaboration should be viewed as either amoral opportunism or the expression of ideological affinity with the Nazis. His résumé of the impact of dekulakization, collectivization, and Stalinist repression in the 1930s as facilitators of a "new type of individual ... who would turn against anyone designated by the authorities as the enemy" (p. 68) may lead the way in understanding, why some were willing to turn against their neighbors, why others were not, and which other factors triggered particular decisions or actions. Furthermore, studying collaboration in the territories of the German-occupied BSSR must conjoin with analyses of its counterpart, the Soviet-led partisan movement. In many cases, locals faced local police staff attempting to enforce German rule by day and partisans requesting support for their cause at night, a conundrum that drove individuals to allegiances with either not because they chose to, but because they were forced to do so literally at gunpoint. The role of other national groups' participation in the campaigns led by occupation authorities ought to be considered as well. Latvian and Lithuanian involvement in, for instance, so-called punitive or anti-partisan operations that often enough ended in the death of hundreds, if not thousands of Belarusians, certainly shine a light on both German and Belarusian agency.

Pointing to dynamics on the chess board to summarize the problem of collaboration in Belarus may not be the best choice if the suggestive metaphor is not used to full capacity. The King is powerful and able to move into any direction, but, just like the Pawn, only one step at a time. Focusing on the Pawn's powerlessness, in turn, might foreclose the search for conditions or instances in which the Pawn assumes the position of a Queen, potentially defeating the King, or for explanations as to why these conditions were never fulfilled. The Pawn kills at an angle, but not forward, and must not go backwards. Does the motive of "once you're in, you're in" really hold true in a situation of occupation violence that triggered other violence as well? The many members of the police who defected to the partisans in 1943 prove otherwise. Nonetheless, considering the neither horizontal, nor vertical direction the Pawns' action may take might reveal an important aspect to further probe in assessing relevant agency and power relations under occupation.

Finally, the chess board houses many pieces and multiple parties, but none of them are the players. An understanding of why some local residents sided with occupation authorities must be open to considering that decisions under duress often have short-term goals in mind, rather than following a fully planned strategy. Just as the German occupiers regularly adjusted their use of "collaborators," the latter made choices that may require us to devise a new vocabulary to understand and represent local responses to the occupation regime.

**Anika Walke**
Washington University in St. Louis


Andrea Graziosi and Frank E. Sysyn (eds.), *Communism and Hunger: The Ukrainian, Kazakh, and Soviet Famines in Comparative Perspective*. Toronto: Canadian Institute of Ukrainian Studies Press, 2016. 158 pp.

Famine is never a wholly natural disaster; it always has a man-made dimension. Andrea Graziosi and Frank E. Sysyn, the editors of the multi-dimensional and thought-provoking *Communism and Hunger: The Ukrainian, Kazakh, and Soviet Famines in Comparative*

*Perspective*, try to convince readers that famines are not only terrifying weapons of war but also powerful engines of economic transformation. Throughout six carefully crafted chapters, specialists in Ukrainian, Kazakh, all-Soviet, and Chinese famines gradually reveal when and why the great twentieth-century famines caused by state policies unfolded. The volume is important for two reasons. It takes as its subject famines in the context of communist development programs, namely Stalin's Great Turning Point and Mao's Great Leap Forward. Moreover, the book is a first attempt to compare not only Soviet and Chinese famines but also Soviet famines with one another. It is a valuable invitation to further research into this overlooked—not to say neglected—topic in academic research.

For many, great historical famines were an immanent part of the development of the capitalist system of the imperial era. In India, China, Egypt, and Ireland (to mention just a few "lands of famine"), many people died while being forcefully incorporated into the economic and political structures of the modern world. The phrase *Communism and Hunger*, as the editors rightly point out in their introduction, would "seem to be a contradiction in terms." Yet, as the studies in the volume suggest, famines were also parts of the socialist experiments—not only in the USSR (1931–33 and 1946–47) and China (1958–62) but also in Ethiopia (1983–85) and North Korea (1994–98). Different chapters in the volume deal with the similarities and differences in the process of unraveling the realities behind famines both within the Soviet Union and China as well as in comparative perspective, exploring their economic and political dimensions. As pointed out by Sarah Cameron in her contribution on the Kazakh Famine (1930–33), "[a] famine is a complex human crisis, the study of which requires a range of methodologies, including social, political, economic, and environmental history" (p. 32). As demonstrated by the contributors, famines also powerfully illuminate not only states' political economies and food regimes but also patterns of organized mass violence and very often much more tangible forms of the cultural responses to disaster connected to the politics of historiography and memory.

Perhaps the most valuable contribution of the volume lies in its comparative design. The book is divided into two parts—the first focusing on study of the Ukrainian Holodomor, Kazakh famine, and the Chinese Great Leap Forward, and the second on the similarities and differences among them (especially in the analysis by Lucien Bianco and Andrea Graziosi). Also, Niccolò Pianciola's analysis stands out as a call for the further examination of the under-studied geographic and environmental dimensions of transnational pastoralism in Inner Asia. Nonetheless, the comparative spirit seems to penetrate each chapter. For example, in his chapter "Food Shortages, Hunger, and Famines in the USSR, 1928–33," Nicholas Werth places the Ukrainian Holodomor within the broader aspect of other "islands of famine" within the USSR—more importantly in the steppe parts of Kazakhstan, the Lower and Middle Volga, and the Central Chernozem regions. In the discussion of the Great Famine in China, Zhou Xun points to the regional distribution, spatial unevenness, and complicated politics of memory—especially in comparison to the Ukrainian Holodomor. Bianco and Graziosi in their respective chapters carefully point out the various similarities and differences between Soviet and Chinese famine catastrophes, exploring more the demographic and economic factors in one case (Bianco's chapter) and more political, ideological, and historiographic dimensions in the other (Graziosi's analysis). The richness and complexities of these chapters showcase the need for further comparative research into the transnational context of socialist famines and the potential influence they may have exerted on one another.

The volume, however, uncovers yet other interesting dimensions of socialist famines, namely both their neglect in Western scholarship and the complicated politics of memory within the analyzed societies. The Ukrainian Holodomor for a very long time was understood as a mere "food shortage" (to use Walter Duranty's phrase); the Kazakh famine was a "miscalculation on the part of Stalin"; and, finally, the Chinese famine is still being called simply the "Three Difficult Years" by many in China. The researchers of socialist famines need to deal not only with scarce resources and the internal politics of the archives but also with the various misrepresentations of the topic—not to say denial—in the West and "blank memory spots" in national historiographies. In this regard, Cameron's and

Xun's chapters stand out in particular as important mirrors that clearly reflect the complicated politics of documents, archives, national memories, and Western scholarship.

*Communism and Hunger: The Ukrainian, Kazakh, and Soviet Famines in Comparative Perspective* is a new and refreshing analysis of famines in the context of socialist experiments. It points to the importance of studying political famines not only in the context of socialist food regimes and political economy broadly speaking, but also as case studies of mass state violence against governments' own citizens. It could be argued that the volume only whets the appetite, and that 158 pages are not enough to provide complete answers for an unfulfilled curiosity about this too often ignored subject. It would also not have been unfruitful for the editors to have incorporated the Ethiopian (1983–85) and North Korean (1994–98) cases into the analysis. Nonetheless, this valuable collection will certainly spur further analysis of political famines in their transnational contexts.

**Karolina Koziura**
PhD Candidate
The New School for Social Research, New York

Mikhail Minakov, *Development and Dystopia: Studies in Post-Soviet Ukraine and Eastern Europe*. Stuttgart: *ibidem*-Verlag, 2018. 280 pp.

With the pro-EU Revolution of Dignity in 2013, Russia's annexation of Crimea and its subsequent hybrid aggression in Eastern Ukraine and beyond, "Ukraine is likely to remain at the center of attention for all major geopolitical centers for the foreseeable future" (p. 243). Moreover, dealing with the opened Pandora's box of discontent and demodernization in CEE states and the Eastern Neighborhood, and safeguarding the future of the EU requires a reflection over the past twenty-five years of modernization efforts, revolutionary cycles, new hopes, and new traumas in post-Soviet space. In his new monograph, Ukrainian political philosopher and social analyst Mikhail Minakov seeks to consider (de)modernization dynamics in Ukrainian politics (also within the wider context of transition studies and

East European Politics), making a special effort to understand the human dimension thereof. Structurally, the book elaborates on four major themes: 1) political ontology and (de)modernization in new East European cultures; 2) the peculiarities and outcomes of Ukraine's revolutionary experiences; 3) the dynamics of Euromaidan and the political transformations it brought about; and 4) the regional perspective and respective worrying security trends.

A lot has been written about the transition experience of post-Soviet states, Ukrainian politics, and Euromaidan, as well as the relationships between the EU, Russia, and other post-Soviet states. However, there are at least five reasons why I would recommend *Development and Dystopia* to both experienced Eastern European and Ukrainian Studies specialists, and those seeking to capture political dynamics in Ukraine and beyond at a glance.

First and foremost, the author excellently conceptualizes a comprehensive set of political developments in Ukraine and Eastern Europe, drawing on critical theory by Jürgen Habermas and modernization theory. Applying to post-Soviet social reality insights into the multi-dimensional nature of modernity, and its temporal and spatial characteristics, Mikhail Minakov argues that there is "a growing tendency of demodernization in Eastern Europe" (p. 22). The author's understanding of the core of the demodernization process is rooted in the interplay between the System (public institutions, such as state, law and law enforcement) and the Lifeworld (private institutions, such as business, consumption patterns, or family life). An important feature of the Soviet "modernization project" was the "dominance of the System" that led to the colonization or "ghettoization" of the Lifeworld (p. 21). Subsequently, according to Minakov, the post-Soviet transition project resulted in "double colonization," where the System continues to be excessively intrusive vis-à-vis the Lifeworld, and the Lifeworld damages the order of the System (p. 11). Thus, the author views the formation of "power verticals," the prominent role of individual oligarchs and financial-political groups (FPGs) in political processes and systemic corruption as key symptoms of reverse tendencies in development in Ukraine and other post-Soviet societies.

This brings me to the second crucial strength of the book. *Development and Dystopia* is exceptionally good at linking the history of political phenomena to their present, as well as explaining the interplay between micro- and macro-level politics. The most striking examples of the former are, to my mind, the author's insights into Ukraine's revolutionary cycles and the history of the "Novorossiya" project. The latter can be exemplified by the author's detailed elaboration on the interlinkages between the micro-politics of FPGs and their macro-level political role, as well as the multi-level review of volunteers' role in the post-Euromaidan state. The above strengths have enabled the author to create a holistic vision of Ukraine and post-Soviet space as "a global historical laboratory for testing demodernization schemes" (p. 11), featuring complex networks of the Public and the Private, the Genuine and the Cosmetic, the Formal and the Informal, and the Soviet and the Post-Soviet.

Third, modern scholarship in transition and development studies tends to explore macro-level phenomena without highlighting human perceptions thereof. *Development and Dystopia* attempts to fill this lacuna by focusing on the human dimension of transition, collective pain, trauma, and *ressentiment* in post-Communist space. According to Minakov, "revenge, mutual punishment and *ressentiment* are all at the center of the dialectics in East European modernity" (p. 53). This statement makes a lot of sense with respect to the results of the author's empirical study of the Euromaidan and Antimaidan activists' perceptions of the EU and Russia, and Ukrainians' perceptions of the "Novorossiya" project, as well as the author's reference to countless "moral panic" incidents in Ukraine (p. 69). The interplay of hope and pain represents the "human face" of the complex post-Soviet transition processes, and conditions the population's extreme vulnerability to news, reform projects, fake news and, consequently, antagonism, far-right nationalism, and hatred. That is why it is extremely important to consider the human perspective—such as traumatic experiences, acting as possible triggers of moral panic—in both scholarship and political decision-making.

It is noteworthy that *Development and Dystopia* distinguishes the far-reaching consequences that Russia's aggressive policy vis-à-vis Ukraine has had for both the Eurasian Economic Union (EAEU) and the EU's Eastern Partnership project. According to Minakov, "before the Crimean and Donbas crises, the two integration projects were expected to support the process of integration between different macro-regions of Big Europe: the EU and the EAEU," with the European Neighborhood Policy (ENP) as a tool for creating "a soft regional integration project moving Eastward" (p. 294). However, Russia's aggression in Ukraine created "dynamic obstacles" to both the idea of "United Europe," and to the deepening of integration under the auspices of Eurasian Union and successful implementation of the Eastern partnership initiative. Distinguishing the "growing gap between two Neighbourhoods" as a security challenge capable of destroying the EU from within, Minakov calls for reforming the EU's strategic approach vis-à-vis the Eastern Neighborhood and Russia, and attempting to bring the "United Europe" idea back to the agenda (pp. 323, 327).

Last, but not least, based on the above mixture of insights and conceptualizations, the book offers three sets of recommendations on promoting modernization in Ukraine and Eastern Europe. The latter includes tackling the gap between the aims and tools of their achievement within the ENP, as well as the EU's developing a three-component approach towards Eastern Europe (general strategy vis-à-vis the post-Soviet countries; country-specific strategies and "a policy towards growing competition and possible cooperation with Russia in the region") (p. 324). Based on Kant's concept of "perpetual peace, Minakov emphasizes the need for "institutional and political infrastructure for peace in prevention of the state of war," putting greater value on people's creativity in the public policy domain, as well as launching a dialogue between intellectuals and political elites (p. 94). With respect to Ukraine, *Development and Dystopia* calls for stricter separation of powers, focus on the implementation of the parliamentary model, the development of SMEs, and revival of the "sobornist" idea of unity in plurality (pp. 238–39).

High-quality conceptual effort, multi-level analysis, first-hand empirical research, and emphases on the human and regional perspectives of post-Soviet transition make *Development and*

*Dystopia* exciting and useful reading for specialists in East European and Ukrainian studies, diplomats and development practitioners, as well as all those seeking to learn more about the political dynamics in the region.

**Maryna Rabinovych**
PhD Candidate
National I.I. Mechnikov University of Odesa

Sander Brouwer (ed.), *Contested Interpretations of the Past in Polish, Russian, and Ukrainian Film: Screen as Battlefield*. Leiden/Boston: Brill Rodopi, 2016. 187 pp.

For a long time now film has been present in the academic debate as an important source for memory studies and as an identity shaping tool. Film is an appealing but also challenging object of study, especially when it comes to its capacity as visual representation of the past. *Contested Interpretations of the Past in Polish, Russian, and Ukrainian Film: Screen as Battlefield* is a notable collection of post-conference articles dedicated to complex issues related to representations of the past in the Polish–Russian–Ukrainian memory triangle. The conference "Suffering, Agency, and Memory in Polish, Russian, and Ukrainian Film," held in March 2012 at the University of Groningen, was itself a part of the research project "Memory at War: Cultural Dynamics in Poland, Russia, and Ukraine," led by Alexander Etkind in 2010–2013. The volume includes contributions by scholars from a number of disciplines. Film studies, cultural studies, and media studies researchers as well as Slavists and anthropologists apply different methodologies and provide findings. The volume is an intriguing example of work in progress in post-socialist studies and is an inspiration for the debate on cinema as a tool, agent, and source in memory studies.

Although all nine chapters are very different, we can spot some key notions and phenomena which the authors circle around. One of the core problems tackled in the volume is the postcolonial perspective on the Central and Eastern European region (Lars

Kristensen, Mirosław Przylipiak, Ewa Mazierska). The contributors to this volume successfully demonstrate that David Chioni Moore's influential argumentation about the applicability of a postcolonial perspective to Eastern Europe can be effectively used to describe the identity shaping process, as well as to illuminate several other concepts depicted in the movies discussed in their studies.

Trauma is another one of the central issues addressed in this volume. It is discussed from different perspectives here: as "foundation trauma" (Olga Briukhovetska); as a cultural trauma of the transition period, highlighted in the cutting-edge paper by Mariëlle W. Wijermars; and as postcolonial trauma, addressed by Mirosław Przylipiak in his chapter covering Polish documentaries on the Smolensk plane crash.

Another very contested matter which the authors focus on is the issue of the historical truthfulness of cinematic representations of the past (Mazierska, Briukhovetska, and Wijermars). They draw our attention to some elements of representations that stray far from the narrative offered by documentary sources or by individual memory. Discussing cinema's relationship to "historical truth" (Briukhovetska), and cinema's "superiority to the official, depersonalized history" (Mazierska), scholars tackle the challenge of examining cinematic narratives about the past that may stand in opposition to source-based narratives.

Language features are another core problem discussed in the volume, especially when it comes to Ukrainian and Belarusian cinema (Vitaly Chernetsky, Olga Briukhovetska). For Ewa Mazierska, language is an element that allows a movie to be assigned a specific—national— narrative. However, as Lars Kristensen's chapter argues, the origins and character of cinematic representation may become more complicated when it comes to co-productions determined also by international financial support and influence. A number of questions regarding identifying cinematic representation as "national" still remain to be addressed. The cinema of the former Soviet republics poses particular issues here, especially when it comes to Ukraine, to mention the most striking example. Is a film made before 1991 a Ukrainian film, or a Soviet film? When it comes to these questions, the experience of the Eastern bloc countries differs from those of the former Soviet republics, whose cinematic traditions raise a particular set of questions about change and (disputable) continuity.

An important topic, but one that is only covered briefly in this volume, is the contextualization of film production. The cinematic context and related governmental memory politics are relatively well examined here, for example by Sander Brouwer, but issues around reception and therefore the real influence of movies on viewers in the long term require further research. For instance, audience survey results are problematic to verify as the Internet has become the most powerful content sharing medium. Film reviews, examined by Ewa Mazierska in this volume, are only one part of a movie's reception and are limited to journalists' and film critics' opinions. They can be perceived as an interesting starting point for further media studies research connected with the debate on the past.

In this volume the authors tend to focus on the content of the movies, while methodological issues frequently remain unclear. The authors apply methodologies drawn from film studies, anthropology, and political science, while neglecting the conceptual approaches to film as historical source developed by Marc Ferro, Pierre Sorlin, and Hayden White. This seems to be a problem related to the mutual recognition of methodological achievements between different disciplines. Another issue relates to the use of Ukrainian-language sources. It would appear that this is not considered essential when analyzing Ukrainian film. This seems problematic, since drawing exclusively upon English- and Russian-language literature and sources on Ukrainian cinema while neglecting these available only in Ukrainian (as in the case of Brouwer's chapter) affects and may determine the interpretation. A minor shortcoming of this volume is connected also with the general problem of using internet sources. Some links provided in the footnotes have expired and are now unavailable.

As regards more general issues, the value of the detailed information about the historical background and social context of the main topic provided in each chapter cannot be overestimated. This aspect of the volume facilitates a useful introduction for a wider group of readers not necessarily familiar with this field of studies.

The volume can therefore serve to promote and inspire further research.

The lack of mutual recognition mentioned by Olga Briukhovetska in the case of Ukrainian and Belarusian cinematic representations of the past seems to be a much more general problem in the Central and Eastern European region. Further research with a view to bridging this gap would be very welcome. Ideally, this would include methodological work aimed at leveling out the proportion between film studies and other research fields, including history, political science, and media studies.

Perceiving screen as a battlefield, as this book's title suggests, is not the only option. Cinema may also become a contact zone and a way to overcome traumatic experience (as Mariëlle W. Wijermars argues in her chapter). Not just feature films, but also testimonies used in documentaries can serve this purpose. The question of whether cinematic representations will be used for reconciliation and not only as tools in memory wars remains open. This volume is certainly a valuable contribution to this debate and helps us to understand the processes whereby different narratives about the past are being established in the region.

**Olga Gontarska**
PhD candidate
The Tadeusz Manteuffel Institute of History
Polish Academy of Sciences

Shaun Walker, *The Long Hangover: Putin's New Russia and the Ghosts of the Past.* Oxford: Oxford University Press, 2018. 278 pp.

In this monograph, Moscow correspondent for the *Guardian* Shaun Walker examines the relationship between Russian national identity, as constituted in the Putin years, and recent political developments in the post-Soviet space. The author argues that a resurgent national idea, focusing on Victory in the Great Patriotic War, has promoted social unity and the return of Russia to the ranks of major world players. However, Walker condemns the problematic collateral effects of this narrative: its facilitation of hostility towards the West, of aggression and domination in Russia's periphery and "near abroad," and of illiberal politics and corruption domestically.

The book is primarily a journalistic account (supplemented by some academic literature) and is based on Walker's extensive reporting experience in the region. His argument can be schematized as follows. In the wake of the collapse of the Soviet Union, the myth of the Great Patriotic War remains the only historical narrative in Russia able to generate a high degree of social consensus. This narrative relates the Victory of good over evil, a triumph dearly bought by individual self-sacrifice and steadfast national unity. Putin recognized the nation-building potential of this myth and elevated it to unprecedented dimensions, but also overlaid it with an emphasis on statehood, sovereignty, and military might. This triumphal narrative, however, requires whitewashing the negative aspects of the war: its inglorious, horrific violence, the extent of collaborationism, and the criminal nature of the Stalinist regime which prosecuted it. Putin sanitizes the memory of the War through the education system, media, and legal-administrative pressures, with the result that its objectionable aspects, as well as the crimes of the Stalinist leadership, remain largely unknown to the Russian public.

In Russia's peripheries, the wider history of oppression (of which the Stalinist period was often a highpoint) is also subject to enforced amnesia. In Chechnya, the memory of tsarist colonization, wartime deportations, and the bloodbath of the two Chechen wars is silenced, to construe Russia as a liberator and benefactor of the republic. In recently-annexed Crimea, the history of the Crimean Tatars (also deported on Stalin's orders) is similarly airbrushed, clashing with both the narrative of a Russian Crimea and of a glorious War. In both cases, as in Russia proper, memory of the War and amnesia of its unpalatable aspects function to legitimate corrupt regimes brutally intolerant of opposition, and hostile to the West.

At the same time, in Ukraine, an opposite, incompatible narrative of the Soviet period and of the events of the Great Patriotic War took root, achieving dominance following the Euromaidan revolution in 2014. In the ensuing confrontations in Crimea and the Donbas, Russian aggression and pro-Russian secessionism were galvanized by the War narrative, which framed the conflict as a new struggle with Western expansionism and fascism. This was seemingly "confirmed" by the symbolism and rhetoric espoused in some Ukrainian quarters. "Ingesting a daily diet of war and fascists and heroic last stands" made men more likely "to pick up a gun and go and fight for real" (227). The turn to Russia in Crimea and the Donbas was further eased by nostalgia for the Soviet Union, although hopes for justice and social renewal were ultimately disappointed. All in all, Walker concludes, "Russia's glorious past has become a national obsession, but a prosperous future still seems a long way off" (253).

Although Walker's arguments will be familiar to students of Russian collective memory, the book is valuable in bringing together a series of exclusive interviews with major players in post-Soviet memory politics. These include the ideologist Aleksandr Dugin, the one-time Donbas rebel leader Igor' Strelkov, the current head and Prime Minister of the Republic of Crimea Sergei Aksenov, Iurii Shukhevich, the deputy behind Ukraine's decommunization laws, and others. Equally importantly, Walker's account integrates the stories of ordinary individuals; the argument is evidenced as much through their voice as through the author's own commentary. Walker goes beyond the all-too-common portrayal of Russians zombified by Kremlin-controlled television, exploring why official narratives fall on fertile ground, a line-of-inquiry both more empathetic and analytically productive. Walker also takes care to maintain balance in his condemnation of the Russian memory regime: he notes both the imperfections of Western memory of the crimes of colonialism, for instance, and the inappropriateness of the Baltic and Ukrainian attempts to deal with the Soviet legacy.

Nonetheless, Walker's balanced approach is not upheld consistently. Alongside its negative effects, the contributions of the War myth to fostering national unity, social solidarity, and meaningful collectivist values are acknowledged in passing but not factored into the assessment. Similarly, Walker does not address the question of why the War myth was "weaponized" in the first place. NATO expansion, Western intervention in the Middle East, the unilateral recognition of Kosovo, appear only as Kremlin excuses justifying its own aggression. The idea that Russia may be acting in defense and in response to these developments, for which the War myth is mobilized, is dismissed out-of-hand. In my opinion, Walker also overstates Putin's personal involvement, and the overall political salience of memory, as in the following assessment of the causes of Crimean annexation: "Putin, in addition to his strategic concerns, could not countenance a Ukraine in which the Soviet period was viewed as an occupation, and the glorious Russian war narrative was turned on its head" (131). There are also some minor imprecisions in the text: "the Soviet Ukrainian republic was expanded" in 1939 (as Walker himself indicates elsewhere), not "after the war" (117). Viktor Yanukovych was not "a petty criminal in the 1970s," but was, as a teenager, convicted in 1967 and 1970 (respectively, of theft and battery) (191).

The book offers an insightful analysis of the new Russian historical narrative, which filled the ideological vacuum left in the wake of the Soviet collapse. A well-written and well-researched account, this book will be a useful introduction to those unfamiliar with the contours of contemporary Russian collective memory.

**Antony Kalashnikov**
DPhil candidate
Nuffield College
University of Oxford

## About the Contributors

ANDREAS UMLAND (Dr.Phil. FU Berlin, Ph.D. Cambridge) is Senior Research Fellow at the Institute for Euro-Atlantic Cooperation in Kyiv, and general editor of the book series *Soviet and Post-Soviet Politics and Society* (*ibidem*-Verlag, 2004–) distributed, since 2014, by Columbia University Press. His articles have appeared in, among other journals, *e-Foreign Affairs, e-Foreign Policy, Political Studies Review, Perspectives on Politics, European Political Science, Journal of Democracy, Europe-Asia Studies, European History Quarterly, Problems of Post-Communism, Communist and Post-Communist Studies, Russian Review, Nationalities Papers, East European Jewish Affairs, Journal of Slavic Military Studies, Demokratizatsiya, Internationale Politik, Österreichische Zeitschrift für Politikwissenschaft, Osteuropa, Jahrbuch für Ostrecht,* and *Voprosy filosofii*.

YULIYA YURCHUK, Ph.D., is a Post-Doctoral Researcher in History at Södertörn University, Sweden. She defended her doctoral dissertation *Reordering of Meaningful Worlds: Memory of the Organization of Ukrainian Nationalists and the Ukrainian Insurgent Army in Post-Soviet Ukraine* in 2015. Her research interests are the history of World War II, memory studies, nationalism, and post-colonial studies.

IGOR BARINOV (Cand. of Sciences in Hist. (Ph.D.) Moscow State University) is Research Fellow at the Institute of World Economy and International Relations of Russian Academy of Sciences in Moscow, and Visiting Scholar at the Herder Institute for Historical Research on East Central Europe in Marburg. His articles have appeared in, among other journals, *Slavyanovedenie, Obshchestvennye nauki i sovremennost', Forum noveishei vostochnoevropeiskoi istorii i kul'tury, Petersburg Historical Journal, Revista de Istoriei a Moldovei,* and *Civitas et Lex*.

IVAN GOMZA is Associate Professor at the National University of "Kyiv-Mohyla Academy" where he teaches courses on social movements, authoritarian regimes, and political extremism. He holds a

Ph.D. from the National University of "Kyiv-Mohyla Academy" where he wrote his thesis on French far-right ideology. He has recently finished editing a book manuscript on the instrumentalization of fears of national decay by the French far right between 1871 and 1945. He has published articles on Ukrainian integral nationalism, contentious politics in Ukraine, and authoritarian regimes in various journals, including *Communist and Post-Communist Studies* and *Journal of Balkan and Near Eastern Studies*.

**SIMON SCHLEGEL** studied social anthropology and Slavic linguistics in Zürich. He moved on to the Max Planck Institute for Social Anthropology in Halle, Germany, where he worked in the research group "Historical Anthropology in Eurasia." He earned his PhD in 2016 with a study about the creation and maintenance of ethnic boundaries in rural southern Ukraine. He is currently a peace worker in Kyiv in a project funded through the Civil Peace Service Program of the German Ministry of Economic Cooperation and Development. He runs a project called "empowering civil society for a transformation of commemorative culture" that uses interviews with victims of the war in Donbas to stimulate public discourse in Ukraine.

**MYROSLAV SHKANDRIJ** (Ph. D, Toronto) is Professor of Slavic Studies at the University of Manitoba. He is the author of, among others, *Modernists, Marxists, and the Nation: The Ukrainian Literary Discussion of the 1920s* (CIUS, 1992); *Russia and Ukraine: Literature and the Discourse of Empire from Napoleonic to Postcolonial Times* (McGill-Queen's University Press, 2001); *The Phenomenon of the Ukrainian Avant-Garde 1910-1935* (Winnipeg Art Gallery, 2002); *Jews in Ukrainian Literature: Representation and Identity* (Yale University Press, 2009); and *Ukrainian Nationalism: Politics, Ideology, and Literature, 1929-1956* (Yale University Press, 2015). His articles have appeared in *Nationalities Papers, Canadian Slavic Studies, Canadian-American Slavic Studies*, and other journals.

Marina M. Lebedeva

# RUSSIAN STUDIES OF INTERNATIONAL RELATIONS

From the Soviet Past to the Post-Cold-War Present

Recently, a renewed international interest in Russia as a world political actor has emerged. Against this background, it is useful to better understand how international relations and foreign affairs are studied in Russia and how future Russian political actors, diplomatic personnel, ministerial bureaucrats, business managers, area experts, and other officials, activists, or researchers are taught for their work on the international arena. What are the theories, approaches, and schools that guide Russian teaching on, and research of, international relations? The current state of Russian studies of International Relations (IR), to a large degree, reflects the history and development of IR research during Soviet times. However, over the past 25 years, one could also observe a number of new developments—both substantive and institutional—which are important not only for properly assessing the new state of this academic discipline in Russia, but also for better comprehending Russian foreign policy as well as various international activities of Russia's regions, businesses, media, etc.

"Lebedeva, perhaps the most outstanding Russian IR specialist, provides us with an in-depth analysis of Russian IR concepts in theoretical and applied research."—Prof. Sergey V. Chugrov, Moscow State Institute of International Relations, Editor-in-Chief of "POLIS: Politicheskie issledovaniia," the journal of the Russian Association of Political Sciences

"The uniqueness of the book is connected with the fact that it is written by one of the most prominent scholars in the field."—Prof. Tatiana Alekseeva, Head of the Department of Political Theory at Moscow State Institute of International Relations

10/2018, 216 p.
Paperback, $40.00
ISBN 978-3-8382-0851-0

e-book, $19.99
ISBN 978-3-8382-6851-4

*ibidem* Press | Leuschnerstr. 40 | 30457 Hannover | Germany
Phone: +49 (0) 511 2 62 22 00 | Fax: +49 (0) 511 2 62 22 00 | sales@ibidem.eu | www.ibidem.eu

*ibidem*

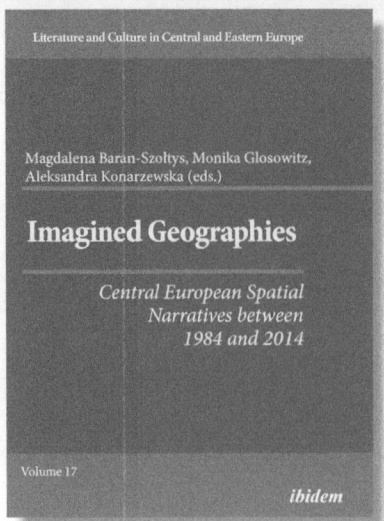

Aleksandra Konarzewska, Monika Glosowitz,
Magdalena Baran-Szoltys (eds.)

# IMAGINED GEOGRAPHIES

Central European Spatial Narratives between 1984 and 2014

In 1984 Czech writer Milan Kundera published his essay 'The Tragedy of Central Europe' in The New York Review of Books, which established the framework for disputes about the space 'between East and West' for the following 30 years. Even today, the echo of those debates is still audible in spatial narratives. Discussing the way in which literary figures are positioned within new hierarchies such as gender, class, or ethnicity, this volume shows how the space of the imagined Central Europe has been de- and reconstructed. Special attention is paid to the role of the past in shaping contemporary spatial discourse.

„What is Central Europe? The discursive field that defines, reflects upon and depicts Central Europe, this collection of essays argues, is literature. Already in the 1980s, Milan Kundera argued that a political accident had moved countries which considered themselves the cultural center of Europe, Poland, the Czech Republic, or even Ukraine, into a political East, the Eastern bloc. The Center of Europe disappeared, and only after the fall of the Berlin Wall it started to reappear, mostly in literary and essayistic writing. The articles in this volume look closely at this writing and show how post-socialist literature moves back in time in order to revive a cultural European center. Nostalgic memories and mythic reveries evoke an image of Central Europe from a time before the world was divided into East and West."—Professor Schamma Schahadat, Institute of Slavic Languages and Literatures, University of Tübingen

**10/2018, 166 p.**
Paperback, $40.00
ISBN 978-3-8382-1225-8

e-book, $22.99
ISBN 978-3-8382-7225-2

*ibidem* Press | Leuschnerstr. 40 | 30457 Hannover | Germany
Phone: +49 (0) 511 2 62 22 00 | Fax: +49 (0) 511 2 62 22 00 | sales@ibidem.eu | www.ibidem.eu

Péter Krekó, Attila Juhász

# THE HUNGARIAN FAR RIGHT
Social Demand, Political Supply, and International Context

This timely book examines far-right politics in Hungary—but its relevance points much beyond Hungary. With its two main players, the radical right Jobbik and populist right Fidesz, it is an essentially Eastern European, European, and global phenomenon. Jobbik and Fidesz, political parties with a populist, nativist, authoritarian approach, Eastern and pro-Russian orientation, and strong anti-Western stance, are on the one hand products of the problematic transformation period that is typical for post-communist countries. But they are products of a "populist Zeitgeist" in the West as well, with declining trust in representative democratic and supranational institutions, politicians, experts, and the mainstream media. The rise of politicians such as Nigel Farage in the UK, Marine Le Pen in France, Norbert Hofer in Austria, and, most notably, Donald Trump in the US are clear indications of this trend. In this book, the story of Jobbik (and Fidesz), contemporary players of the Hungarian radical right scene, are not treated as separate case studies, but as representatives of broader international political trends. Far-right parties such as Jobbik (and increasingly Fidesz) are not pathologic and extraordinary, but exaggerated, seemingly pathological manifestations of normal, mainstream politics. The radical right is not the opposite and denial of the mainstream, but the sharp caricature of the changing national, and often international mainstream.

„The Hungarian Far Right provides a detailed analysis of the unique ideas, values, voters, organizational strategy, and international alliances of the Jobbik party and its allied movement. Krekó and Juhász show that its voter base is primarily middle-class young people worried about their social status, not the losers of transition. They expose the uniquely Hungarian features of the ideology, including its myth of cultural affinity with Eastern peoples, and the nature of Jobbik's alliances with Iran and Russia. This is a must read for those interested in analyzing and resisting the rise and mainstreaming of far right movements in Europe."—Mitchell A Orenstein, Professor and Chair of Russian and East European Studies, University of Pennsylvania

10/2017, 268 p.
Paperback, $40.00
ISBN 978-3-8382-1184-8

e-book, $24.99
ISBN 978-3-8382-7074-6

*ibidem* Press | Leuschnerstr. 40 | 30457 Hannover | Germany
Phone: +49 (0) 511 2 62 22 00 | Fax: +49 (0) 511 2 62 22 00 | sales@ibidem.eu | www.ibidem.eu

Abel Polese

# THE SCOPUS DIARIES AND THE (IL)LOGICS OF ACADEMIC SURVIVAL

A Short Guide to Design Your Own Strategy And Survive Bibliometrics, Conferences, and Unreal Expectations in Academia

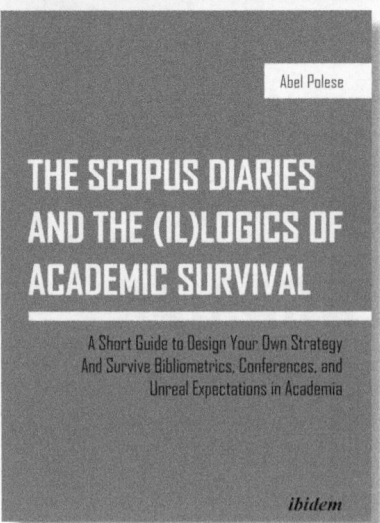

Now that academics are required to be teachers, managers, media catalyzers, analysts, fundraisers, and social media animals: How do you strike a good balance between what is expected from you and what you want to do? What conferences to attend? How to find the money to go there? Is it worth it to act as a peer reviewer? What publishers are best to target? Is publishing a chapter in an edited book worth the work? This book is intended to help scholars to design and think strategically about their own career. Beginning with "How to get published in good journals," it explores a number of questions that most academics encounter at various stages of their careers.

"Polese's demystification of peer review and the high-stakes gambit of academic publishing is well overdue. He lifts the lid on both overall strategies and the no less important nitty-gritty aspects."—Jeremy Morris, Aarhus University

"This is a must-read if you are in academia and do not yet have a tenured position. Even more urgently, it is a must-read for everyone who wants to or should have to reflect on the complex and sometimes counter-productive logics of today's (social) science production."—Heiko Pleines, Professor of Comparative Politics at the University of Bremen, Germany

"The Scopus Diaries is an indispensable guide for early researchers who often find it difficult to balance academic life with their non-academic passion. If offers a vision of work-life balance from one of the best in the field. A must-read primer for non-Western scholars interested in learning about the academic strategies in the West."—Rajan Kumar, Jahawaral Nehru University India

"The neoliberalised university thrives on metrics, performances, citations, and research income. Modern academics have to reluctantly navigate these waters and this can be a daunting task, particularly for those at the early stages of their careers. The Scopus Diaries will help them in this endeavour through a series of precious tips and strategies that most researchers wished they knew about when they started a PhD."—Filippo Menga, University of Reading and Scopus Early Career Researcher UK Award Winner for 2018 (Social Sciences)

"Abel Polese has acquired an unrivalled understanding of how academia works and has now distilled his insights to provide an indispensable guide to navigate through the maze. The only mystery is why he has decided to share this precious insider information. My advice is to grab a copy before he reconsiders."—Donnacha Ó Beacháin, Dublin City University

10/2018, 232 p.
Paperback, $25.00
ISBN 978-3-8382-1199-2

e-book, $6.99
ISBN 978-3-8382-7199-6

*ibidem* Press | Leuschnerstr. 40 | 30457 Hannover | Germany
Phone: +49 (0) 511 2 62 22 00 | Fax: +49 (0) 511 2 62 22 00 | sales@ibidem.eu | www.ibidem.eu

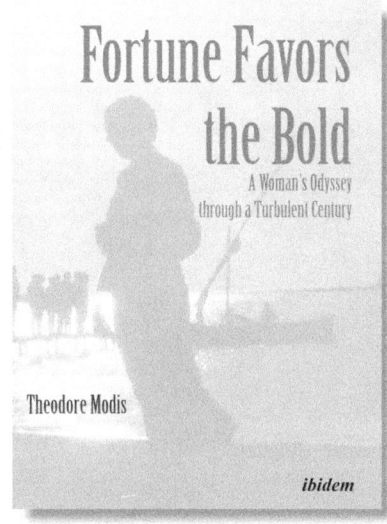

Theodore Modis

# FORTUNE FAVORS THE BOLD
## A Woman's Odyssey through a Turbulent Century

In the early twentieth century, a teenage Greek girl in Constantinople loses both her parents and, together with her younger sister, gets thrown into a massive population exchange between Greece and Turkey. She ends up in a refugee camp in northern Greece. With determination she creates a life in her new country, becoming a teacher in a small mountain town near Greece's northwestern borders with Albania and Yugoslavia. She meets and marries a young lawyer from a historic and tragic Macedonian family. Her story extends through a century of war and peace and is peppered with likable characters, horrific events, and a love story. Among the protagonists are two strong women, a charming and indomitable man, and a smart but sickly kid. Now and again her drive, perseverance, and common sense will save the day and reward her with happiness, which nevertheless will come and go like interludes of sunshine in otherwise endlessly stormy weather. The reader will also get candid and authentic glimpses on poorly known historical conflicts such as the Balkan Wars, the world's greatest ethnic cleansing, the occupation loan that the Nazis exacted from Greece, the Greek Civil War, the Turkish invasion of Cyprus, and the dispute over the use of the name Macedonia.

"A woman's amazing life"—Nicholas A. Gage, author of bestseller *Eleni*

"A remarkable, moving, and informative story. A must read for anyone with an interest in Greece or simply in human nature."—Athanasios G. Konstandopoulos, Chairman of the Board and Managing Director, Center for Research and Technology Hellas

"This fascinating family saga brought to life a region and events that I knew little about. I highly recommend it."—Joe McMahon, author of *The Face of God*

"A heartbreaking yet endearing look at the realities of war for one couple and their family, this novel proves the simple bonds of education and family are the strongest. It is a unique human-interest piece, showing everyday Greek life before, during, and after WWII."—InD'tale Magazine

**10/2018, 404 p.**
Paperback, $25.00
ISBN 978-3-8382-1197-8

*ibidem* Press | Leuschnerstr. 40 | 30457 Hannover | Germany
Phone: +49 (0) 511 2 62 22 00 | Fax: +49 (0) 511 2 62 22 00 | sales@ibidem.eu | www.ibidem.eu

*ibidem*

*ibidem*.eu